IMAGES OF WAR

HIMMLER'S DEATH SQUAD

EINSATZGRUPPEN IN ACTION, 1939–1945

RARE PHOTOGRAPHS FROM WARTIME ARCHIVES

Ian Baxter

Pen & Sword
MILITARY

First published in Great Britain in 2021 by
PEN & SWORD MILITARY
an imprint of
Pen & Sword Books Ltd
47 Church Street
Barnsley
South Yorkshire
S70 2AS

ISBN 978-1-52677-856-7

Typeset by Concept, Huddersfield, West Yorkshire HD4 5JL
Printed and bound in England by CPI Group (UK) Ltd, Croydon CR0 4YY

Pen & Sword Books Limited incorporates the imprints of Atlas, Archaeology, Aviation, Discovery, Family History, Fiction, History, Maritime, Military, Military Classics, Politics, Select, Transport, True Crime, Air World, Frontline Publishing, Leo Cooper, Remember When, Seaforth Publishing, The Praetorian Press, Wharncliffe Local History, Wharncliffe Transport, Wharncliffe True Crime and White Owl.

For a complete list of Pen & Sword titles please contact
PEN & SWORD BOOKS LIMITED
47 Church Street, Barnsley, South Yorkshire S70 2AS, England
E-mail: enquiries@pen-and-sword.co.uk
Website: www.pen-and-sword.co.uk

Contents

Introduction 5

Formation 7

Chapter One
Murder in Poland 11

Chapter Two
Murder in Russia 43

Chapter Three
Murder in the Baltic States 73

Chapter Four
Last Years 89

Epilogue 95

Appendix 1
Structure of the Reich Main Security Office 117

Appendix 2
Einsatzgruppen operations in Poland 119

Appendix 3
Einsatzgruppen task force on the Eastern Front 121

Appendix 4
Number of people killed by the Einsatzgruppen 125

Appendix 5
German Police Battalions and Regiments, 1939–44 127

Appendix 6
Executions carried out by Einsatzkommando 3 129

About the Author

Ian Baxter is a military historian who specialises in German twentieth-century military history. He has written more than fifty books including *Poland – The Eighteen Day Victory March*, *Panzers In North Africa*, *The Ardennes Offensive*, *The Western Campaign*, *The 12th SS Panzer-Division Hitlerjugend*, *The Waffen-SS on the Western Front*, *The Waffen-SS on the Eastern Front*, *The Red Army at Stalingrad*, *Elite German Forces of World War II*, *Armoured Warfare*, *German Tanks of War*, *Blitzkrieg*, *Panzer-Divisions at War*, *Hitler's Panzers*, *German Armoured Vehicles of World War Two*, *Last Two Years of the Waffen-SS at War*, *German Soldier Uniforms and Insignia*, *German Guns of the Third Reich*, *Defeat to Retreat: The Last Years of the German Army At War 1943–45*, *Operation Bagration – the Destruction of Army Group Centre*, *German Guns of the Third Reich*, *Rommel and the Afrika Korps*, *U-Boat War*, and most recently *The Sixth Army and the Road to Stalingrad*. He has written over a hundred articles including 'Last days of Hitler', 'Wolf's Lair', 'The Story of the V1 and V2 Rocket Programme', 'Secret Aircraft of World War Two', 'Rommel at Tobruk', 'Hitler's War With his Generals', 'Secret British Plans to Assassinate Hitler', 'The SS at Arnhem', 'Hitlerjugend', 'Battle of Caen 1944', 'Gebirgsjäger at War', 'Panzer Crews', 'Hitlerjugend Guerrillas', 'Last Battles in the East', 'The Battle of Berlin', and many more. He has also reviewed numerous military studies for publication, supplied thousands of photographs and important documents to various publishers and film production companies worldwide, and lectures to various schools, colleges and universities throughout the United Kingdom and the Republic of Ireland.

Introduction

'In this case the defendants are not simply accused of planning or directing wholesale killings through channels. They are not charged with sitting in an office hundreds and thousands of miles away from the slaughter. It is asserted with particularity that these men were in the field actively superintending, controlling, directing, and taking an active part in the bloody harvest.'

(Nuremburg War Crimes Court, 29 July 1947)

The Einsatzgruppen (literally, task forces) were SS paramilitary death squads that were responsible for mass murder on a mammoth scale mainly across eastern Europe between 1939 and 1942. They were Himmler's murder squads.

Led by Otto Ohlendorf, their personnel came mostly from the Security Police and other security services and the SS. Together they massacred partisans, gypsies, Jews, 'intelligentsia', members of the priesthood, and anyone else they deemed hostile to the Reich. They operated in territories recently occupied by the German army as it advanced through Poland and the Soviet Union, working hand-in-hand with the Order Police battalions, various security police units, foreign auxiliary personnel, Waffen-SS and even regular German soldiers. This book shows how they carried out these brutal 'cleansing' actions, ranging from small isolated killings to mass murders.

Using rare photos, some previously unpublished, together with captions and text, the book shows how Himmler's murder squads played a leading role in the implementation of the 'Final Solution'. It depicts how these murder squads, supported by other personnel, killed more than 2 million people, over a million of whom were Jews, and it helps us understand how even ordinary soldiers and policemen became conditioned to carry out mass murder.

Formation

The Einsatzgruppen were formed under the direction of the SS under the leadership of SS-Obergruppenführer Reinhard Heydrich in March 1938, following the annexation of Austria. They were created from *ad hoc* Einsatzkommando truppen and were responsible for securing government buildings and documents. Originally the Einsatzkommando were part of the Sicherheitspolizei (Security Police or SiPo) which were the state political and criminal investigation agencies. Heydrich was put in charge of the SiPo. He was already responsible for the Sicherheitsdienst (Security Service or SD) and Gestapo.

Over a period of time the security agencies were separated into two groups comprising the Ordnungspolizei (Order Police or Orpo), consisting of both the national uniformed police and the municipal police, along with the Security Police. The Security Police was made up of the combined forces of the Gestapo and the Kriminalpolizei (Kripo).

The Einsatzgruppen were formed under the command of the SS from the SiPo and the SD. In October 1938 two units of Einsatzgruppen were stationed in the German-speaking part of Czechoslovakia known as the Sudetenland. When military action turned out not to be necessary, the Einsatzgruppen were given the task of removing all government papers and police documents. They also surrounded and raided government buildings, detained and questioned senior civil servants, and arrested over 10,000 Czech and German communists.

In September 1939, just as German forces were on the brink of defeating Poland, the Reich Main Security Office (Reichssicherheitshauptamt or RSHA) was established, The office was subordinate to Himmler, and combined the SS Intelligence Service, Gestapo, Criminal Police, and Foreign Intelligence Service into an enormous centralised organization under one roof. It was created to terrorise the entire continent of Europe, and conduct mass murder on a scale never before equalled in history.

As a result of this amalgamation the RSHA obtained overall command of the Einsatzgruppen units, and within days more members were recruited from the echelons of the SS, the SD and the police. However, Heydrich had wasted no time in putting the Einsatzgruppen to use even before the RSHA had taken control. He had planned that they would follow in the wake of the armies as they drove into Poland. Heydrich placed SS-Obergruppenführer Werner Best in command. Before taking his job in the SD, Best had headed Department 1 of the RSHA: Administration and Legal, and had initiated a registry of all Jews in Germany. He assigned Hans-Joachim Tesmer to choose personnel for the Einsatzkommandos. They were to be educated people with military experience, with some members recruited from paramilitary groups such as the Freikorps. They were taught about enemies of the state and indoctrinated in the SS philosophy of racial superiority. All were required to possess a fanatical determination to serve National Socialism with blind allegiance. Poland would be their first blooding.

(**Below**) Himmler appears to be reviewing a unit of SS troops. Pictured to his left is Gottlob Berger. Himmler wanted to build a killing squad that would carry out a reign of terror during military campaigns in the East using special units of the Security Police and SD. These units would accompany the army into foreign territory and combat elements hostile to Germany behind enemy lines of the regular troops. These mobile police formations would be known as the Einsatzgruppen.

(**Opposite, above**) SS-Reichsführer Heinrich Himmler (centre) of the SS was one of the most powerful men in Nazi Germany. He was also the main architect of the Holocaust and directed the murder of millions of innocent people due to his extreme racial and political views.

(**Opposite, below**) SS-Obergruppenführer Reinhard Heydrich. The Einsatzgruppen were formed under the direction of the SS under the leadership of Heydrich. Most of the commanders and officers came from Heydrich's own SD, which comprised many intellectuals from the Security Police and the SS.

(**Above, left**) Walter Friedrich Schellenberg became one of the highest ranking men in the Sicherheitsdienst (SD), eventually becoming head of foreign intelligence. It was Schellenberg who negotiated with the Wehrmacht to obtain logistical support for the Einsatzgruppen. He acted on Heydrich's behalf and issued orders preventing Jews from emigrating out of German-controlled territory.

(**Above, right**) SS-Brigadeführer Otto Ohlendorf was an economist by education and became head of the SD. In 1941 he was appointed commander of Einsatzgruppe D which perpetrated mass murder in Moldova, south Ukraine and the Crimea during 1942.

(**Right**) SS-Gruppenführer Arthur Nebe was a key functionary in the security police. He rose through the ranks of the Prussian police force to become head of the Nazi Criminal Police (Krimialpolizei/Kripo) in 1936, which was amalgamated into the Reich Main Security Office (RSHA) in 1939. Before the 1941 invasion of Russia in June 1941, Nebe volunteered to serve as commanding officer of Einsatzgruppe B, one of the four murder squads used in the rear areas of the Wehrmacht's advance.

Chapter One

Murder in Poland

When the German army advanced into Poland on 1 September 1939, bewildered Polish commanders struggled desperately to hold their forces together. The Polish Army's withdrawal was not a panic flight. It was a kind of stubborn retreat. Villages and towns in the objective area were strongly held by a mixture of Polish troops and partisans, and guerrilla warfare broke out in many places. German soldiers became nervous about the progress of the 'legendary march', and so if shots were fired at them from a village in bandit country, they torched houses, razed villages, and the inhabitants, innocent as well as guilty, found themselves facing firing squads. Surrendered Polish soldiers in uniform were usually shot.

However, even more sinister activities were beginning to generate terror. Behind the regular German army lurked the SS Death Head groups or Totenkopfverbande under the command of Theodor Eicke. Three regiments had been deployed: SS Oberbayern, Brandenburg, and Thuringen. Eicke's men quickly gained a reputation, torturing and killing Poles regarded as hostile to the Reich.

The German army were fully aware of the systematic campaign of slaughter in the rear areas. A few regular soldiers and commanders became uneasy, and some actually complained to their superiors, but nothing was done to stop the killing.

Now Heydrich released the Einsatzgruppen into the rear areas for the first time. In a series of meetings held in August 1939, he had explained that the mission of the Einsatzgruppen would be to kill members of the Polish leadership. This would include the intelligentsia, teachers, the clergy and nobility. As Hitler said, 'There must be no Polish leaders. Where Polish leaders exist they must be killed, however harsh that sounds.' Using dossiers collected by the SD, lists were drawn up of the people to be killed in Poland.

For this the Einsatzgruppen were tasked not with employing their military capabilities but instead terrorizing the civilian population through acts that included hunting down straggling Polish soldiers, confiscating livestock and agricultural produce, and torturing and murdering public figures such as Polish political leaders, business men, priests and intellectuals.

Initially the Einsatzgruppen numbered 2,700 men, and by the time they were sent to Poland that figure had risen to 4,250.

Their mission was 'cleansing and security measures' and their activities in Poland would give the Poles a fitting introduction to the character of German rule. The Einsatzgruppen operations received the cover name 'Tannenberg'.

As the Einsatzgruppen roamed the countryside they searched houses, secured areas, and arrested and summarily shot anyone they deemed suspicious. The mentally ill and the disabled, including patients recuperating in hospitals, were murdered.

In Sladow, 252 PoWs were shot or drowned; at Ciepielow some 300 PoWs were killed; and at Zambrow a further 300 were murdered. Polish PoWs of Jewish origin were regularly selected and executed.

The Wehrmacht leadership did seek to discourage so-called 'wild' shootings, where troops would kill civilians on their own initiative. In fact there were court-martial proceedings against some junior officers who had led these shootings. But this was nullified on 4 October 1939 when Hitler pardoned all military personnel who had been involved in war crimes in Poland.

By the end of the campaign in Poland, it was estimated that some 531 towns and villages had been burned, there had been 714 mass executions, as well as many random incidents of plunder, banditry and murder.

Following the conquering of Poland, a forced euthanasia programme began almost immediately, known as Action T4. This was the murder of all persons with physical or mental disabilities. The Einsatzgruppen were initially tasked with these killings.

At the end of 1939 a second phase of the Operation Tannenberg began, another cleansing action in Poland using the Einsatzgruppen. In Pomerania, a period of more or less unrestrained terror continued in which some 40,000 Poles, including children, were killed.

By 1940, with large areas of Poland now incorporated into the Reich, the final task of the Einsatzgruppen was to round up the remaining Jews and concentrate them in the ghetto system that was being established in major cities and towns. To alleviate the burden of 'dumping' them in overcrowded ghettos, tens of thousands of men, women and children, were driven east into the Soviet Union.

(**Opposite, above**) On 1 September 1939 the Germany army invaded Poland. This photograph shows a Pz.Kpfw.I rolling into a Polish town with the locals watching from the side of the road. This was the first time German soldiers had experienced the east. They had been told that Poles were an inferior race and the Jews should be removed from normal life.

(**Opposite, below**) A column of Pz.Kpfw.IIs rolls through a captured Polish town watched by local members of a Jewish community who can be seen standing at the side of the road. In the wake of these advancing columns were special police units that assisted the new murder squads, or Einsatzgruppen. As they roamed the countryside, villages, towns and cities, these squads were to bring a reign of terror.

(**Above**) Soldiers pause in their advance next to a halted Pz.Kpfw.35(t) in a village. The advance through Poland was rapid and the German war machine captured large areas of the country within days.

(**Opposite, above**) As more areas in Poland were captured, rear German police units moved into the towns and cities and began interrogating people. They segregated Jews, emigrants, Jehovah's Witnesses, gypsies, 'the intelligentsia', and priests. In this photograph German police or soldiers check the identification papers of a Jew in the streets of Krakow.

(**Opposite, below**) A Jewish gentleman is being interrogated by members of the police with the assistance of the Wehrmacht.

(**Opposite, above**) Wehrmacht security soldiers can be seen instructing men and women inside a Polish town. Often Jews were herded from their homes and, with the assistance of the German Police, Wehrmacht and SS, Einsatzgruppen units would round them up and murder them.

(**Opposite, below**) Jewish men being escorted along a road through a town. Following the German invasion of Poland there followed a period of more or less unrestrained terror in the country, particularly in the incorporated territories.

(**Above**) Jewish gentlemen have been rounded up by a Wehrmacht security unit; their fate can be only imagined.

(**Above**) A frightened Polish man is being searched by a German soldier during the invasion of Poland in September 1939.

(**Opposite, above**) Following the capture of Bydgoszcz between 3 and 4 September 1939, Einsatzgruppen, SS units and Wehrmacht soldiers assisting in the operation killed 1,200–3,000 Polish civilians in retaliation for sniper attacks on German military units following the capture of the city. The mass execution became known as the Valley of Death. The murdered included the president of Bydgoszcz, Leon Barciszewski, and fifty Polish prisoners of war from Bydgoszcz. This photograph shows civilians being rounded up and executed.

(**Opposite, below**) A priest along with civilians from Bydgoszcz have been rounded up. More than 20,000 Polish citizens of Bydgoszcz were either shot or died in concentration camps during the occupation.

(**Above**) A typical photograph of murder during the invasion of Poland. Here a group of Poles have been rounded up and executed by an Einsatzgruppen unit. Note that they are standing inside their own grave, which probably suggests they were forced to dig it first before being killed.

(**Opposite, above**) German soldiers on the march during the initial phase of the campaign. During the Wehrmacht's drive through Poland, the individual German soldier was often responsible for indiscriminate shootings. The army leadership did not promote these acts of violence against innocent civilians, discouraging so-called 'wild' shootings, there were some court-martial proceedings against junior officers who had led these shootings. But on 4 October 1939 Hitler pardoned all military personnel who had been involved in war crimes in Poland.

(**Opposite, below**) Poles are executed by an Einsatzgruppen unit in October 1939. Following the capture of Poland, the Germans, notably the death squads, went on a rampage of murder and terror, trying to kill as many Jews as possible including those that were regarded hostile to the Reich.

Polish men have been arrested and are being escorted by a Wehrmacht soldier. Often the German army assisted both the SS and Einsatzgruppen in the murder of Jews.

A Wehrmacht security unit has entered a Polish town and the local folk are being collected. They are either being transported to the new ghetto system or led away and murdered.

German police unload frightened and bewildered Jewish gentlemen from a transport. They each carry a loaf of bread and it is more than likely this photograph was taken during a resettlement action.

A policeman poses for the camera during the rounding up of Jews inside a town following the invasion of Poland.

Two photographs taken in sequence showing Jewish men forced to clear up an area of a town that has received significant bomb damage during the invasion of Poland.

Einsatzgruppen during a cleansing action of a town. They have forced some of the men folk against a wall and are in the process of shooting them. One man, on the far right, has turned in fear and faces his murderers.

Polish civilians have been rounded up by Einsatzgruppen and are marched along a road.

(**Above & opposite, above**) Two photographs taken in sequence showing Polish PoWs who have been murdered. Some 300 were rounded up by soldiers of the German 15th Motorised Infantry Regiment in what became known as the Ciepielów massacre on 9 September.

(**Opposite, below**) Male civilians inside a Polish town have been forced against a wall and executed. There were numerous stories of massacres in which soldiers gave their reasons for their barbaric killings. In one, soldiers threw hand grenades into a school building. They said that the teachers and children were harbouring Polish PoWs.

(**Above**) Wehrmacht soldiers enter a Polish town and observe the aftermath of a cleansing action by the Einsatz-gruppen. Piles of bodies can be seen heaped along a road following their execution.

(**Opposite, above**) Jewish people have been rounded up and loaded onto a vehicle during what the Germans often called resettlement actions. In some of these operations, however, Jews were simply herded out into surrounding forests and murdered in pits.

(**Opposite, below**) German soldiers converse with a group of Polish civilians during their drive through Poland. Most of the German advance was unhindered by partisan activity, but some units still decided to burn 531 towns and villages.

(**Above**) A typical scene during the cleansing of the rear areas by the Einsatzgruppen. Here a soldier escorts civilians in file to a spot where they are executed.

(**Opposite**) Inside a forest clearing and a pit has been dug for the execution of what was probably the inhabitants of a nearby town. The photographs depict a policeman armed with a rifle and he can be seen murdering a defenceless female at point blank range.

(**Below**) A Wehrmacht column of support vehicles operating in Poland. Some German infantry units supported the Einsatzgruppen providing logistical support for their operations, and participated in the mass killings.

A Trawniki guard poses for the camera. These men were central and eastern European collaborators who were recruited from Russian PoW camps. While some served in a military capacity, others played an instrumental role in the holocaust, rounding up and transporting Jews from the ghettos to the concentration camps. They also assisted rounding up Jews for the Einsatzgruppen.

The first of five photographs showing Heinrich Himmler at a Trawniki training camp. The duties of these new recruits consisted of supporting the local police units, carrying out deportations and mass executions of Jews.

(**Above**) A graphic scene showing old folk being forced to undress by police and Trawniki men before being led away and murdered in nearby pits.

(**Opposite, above**) German police during a 'resettlement' inside a Polish town escort a Jewish gentleman to an area for transportation.

(**Opposite, below**) During the liquidation of the Krakow ghetto. German police can be seen with a line of murdered civilians who were killed for allegedly resisting the action. In the Krakow ghetto, due to its size the liquidation was done in phases. The first transport consisted of 7,000, the second, 4,000 Jews, all of which were deported to the Belzec death camp in the summer of 1942. It was not until March 1943 that the final liquidation of the ghetto was carried out. Those deemed unfit for labour, which was around 2,000, were rounded up and either murdered in the streets of the ghetto or transported to Auschwitz. The 8,000 Jews that were left were transported and forced to work in the Płaszów Labour camp.

A Wehrmacht motorcyclist more than likely on reconnaissance has halted inside a village surrounded by peasant folk. Often army units arrived in villages and towns searching for Jews and rounded them up for the Einsatzgruppen.

A public execution of Polish hostages in Bydgoszcz, Poland. The image shows the fear in some of the men, with one pleading for his life.

German police and auxiliaries in civilian clothing prepare to execute naked Jewish men and boys who are being lined up at the edge of a mass grave. *(USHMM, Jacob Igra)*

The original caption in Polish reads: From a series of Nazi crimes during the occupation of Poland. The forest near Bochnia. Execution in the forest. *(USHMM, Jacob Igra)*

(**Opposite, above**) German police pose for the camera following the capture of three men who were probably arrested for hostile acts against the German forces during the Polish invasion. All three men would be executed without trial.

(**Opposite, below**) This photograph shows members of the Einsatzgruppen escorting Jewish females through the Kampinos Forest near the village of Palmiry north-west of Warsaw to be murdered in what was known as the Palmiry massacre. These killings took place on 7 and 8 December 1939, when 70 and 80 people were murdered respectively.

(**Above**) This photograph depicts SD personnel during a series of arrests in Łapanka in occupied Poland.

A Wehrmacht soldier escorts Russian prisoners to the rear of the battlefield. Often Soviet prisoners were led away and killed or handed over to the Einsatzgruppen task forces, where they murdered them instead.

Chapter Two

Murder in Russia

For the Nazi empire, a war against Russia entailed a transition from one policy of murder to another. Hitler explained to his generals just before the invasion that the war would be no normal war; it was an 'ideological war of extermination'. In the eyes of Hitler the Soviet Union represented the home of Bolshevism and international Jewry; both had to be rooted out and destroyed.

To deal with enemies in Russia four Einsatzgruppen were used, each numbering 500–990 men, to comprise a total force of 3,000. The units were divided into A, B, C and D and were under the operational control of the higher SS police chiefs in their zones. The first three groups were attached to Army Group North, Centre and South, while D was assigned to the 11th Army. Einsatzgruppe A was directed through Latvia, Lithuania, towards the east. B operated in the direction of Moscow in the area adjoining A to the south. Here it swept the Bezirk Bialystok area for Jews. Across the whole zone of operations, units conducted mass shootings and public hangings. Later B moved to Smolensk and operated in Bobruisk, Gomel, Roslavl and Klintsy, then it moved to Vitebsk, Polotzk, Nevel, Lepel, and Surazh. The command then progressed to Vtasma, and from there they killed the Jewish communities of Gzhatsk and Mozhaisk in the vicinity of Moscow. The actions were fast and effective to prevent the Jews from escaping the advancing army. To the south and east of Smolensk and Minsk, two Sonderkommandos murdered everyone in their wake from Velikiye, Luki, Kalinin, Orsha, Gomel, to Orel and Kursk. .

Further south, in the Ukraine, advancing simultaneously, was Einsatzgruppe C. It conducted shootings and hangings in and around Lviv, Lutsk, Rovno, Zhytomyr, Pereyaslav, Yagotyn, Lubny, Kiev, Rostov, Tarnopol and Kharkov. In a year it had murdered 60,000 people.

Einsatzgruppe D operated in the Crimea. It conducted extensive killing actions in northern Transylvania, Cernauti, Kishinev, and across the whole region including the Peninsula.

As with other units of the Einsatzgruppen they liquidated not only Jews but communist leaders, partisans and other elements they deemed undesirable to the Reich. The killing squads gave no reason for their actions and would comb the rear areas extensively killing anyone.

One of the daily operational reports, of which some 200 were submitted between July 1941 and April 1942, read:

Chief of the Security Police and the SD
Berlin, July 12, 1941
12 copies (11th copy)
Operational Situation Report USSR No. 20
Einsatzgruppe B:
Location: Minsk

The industrialized areas are only slightly damaged. The town is without light and water. Political and government officials have fled. The population is very depressed. Many people have lost their shelter and the food situation is worsening. To protect the communication lines and prevent acts of sabotage, the Field Commander ordered the arrest of all male inhabitants between the ages of 18–45. The civil prisoners are being screened at this time. The attitude of the population toward the Germans is one of wait-and-see. The Byelorussians show a friendlier attitude towards the Germans. However, the entire population hopes that the occupation will enable them to live a normal life in the near future.

According to the last report, wooden houses in the western part of Minsk were set afire. Apparently the houses were set on fire by Jews because the Jews were supposed to evacuate their homes for returning Byelorussian refugees. At present the population is in a mood to launch a pogrom. Their fury caused certain anti-Jewish actions. A number of Jews were liquidated for this act.

Another sent on 19 July 1941 stated:

Einsatzgruppe B:
Location: Minsk

A meeting of the commander of the Rear Army Area 102 with the higher SS and Police Leader has resulted in complete agreement concerning our further activities. The rear security divisions attach great importance to cooperation with the security police. Liquidation continues daily. If they are not caught red-handed, persons are liquidated according to lists. It has been repeatedly observed that Jews escape into the forests now and try to hide there. The employed White Russians have shown little activity so far. It has been explained already to Dr. Tschora what is expected from their support, particularly concerning the cooperation in the apprehension of Communists, officials, commissars, intellectuals, Jews, etc.

In Minsk Einsatzgruppe B murdered all the civilian prisoners in the camps amounting to some 733 men. In the nearby town of Vitebsk 70–80 people were killed. On both occasions a trench was dug and persons destined to die were placed in front and shot in the back of the neck.

Following the capture of Kiev, Einsatzgruppe C plastered posters all around the city and surrounding villages which read:

Kikes [Jews] of the city of Kiev and vicinity! On Monday, 29 September, you are to appear by 7:00 A.M. with your possessions, money, documents, valuables and warm clothing at Dorogozhitshaya Street, next to the Jewish cemetery. Failure to appear is punishable by death.

Once the Jews had congregated that morning, they were marched to Babi Yar, a ravine 2 miles from the city centre. A truck driver at the scene described what he saw:

I watched what happened when the Jews – men, women and children – arrived. The Ukrainians led them past a number of different places where one after another they had to remove their luggage, then their coats, shoes, and over-garments and also underwear. They had to leave their valuables in a designated place. There was a special pile for each article of clothing. It all happened very quickly … I don't think it was even a minute from the time each Jew took off his coat before he was standing there completely naked …

Once undressed, the Jews were led into the ravine which was about 150m long and 30m wide and a good 15m deep … When they reached the bottom of the ravine they were seized by members of the Schutzpolizei and made to lie down on top of Jews who had already been shot. That all happened very quickly. The corpses were literally in layers. A police marksman came along and shot each Jew in the neck with a submachine gun … I saw these marksmen stand on layers of corpses and shoot one after the other … The marksman would walk across the bodies of the executed Jews to the next Jew who had meanwhile lain down and shoot him.

Over the next week more than 33,000 Jews were murdered at Babi Yar. Over the following months, Babi Yar remained in use as an execution site for gypsies and Soviet prisoners of war. Similar executions occurred in other places in the Soviet Union.

Einsatzgruppe D noted that within nine months of operations its force had killed more than 90,000 people. It boasted an average of 340 persons per day, mostly Jews, gypsies, Asiatics, and 'undesirables'. Between 16 November and 15 December 1941 it averaged 700 a day. A report of April 1942 stated:

The Crimea is freed of Jews. Only occasionally some small groups are turning up, especially in the northern areas. In cases where single Jews could camouflage themselves by means of forged papers, etc, they will, nevertheless, be recognized sooner or later, as experience has taught.

On 14 November 1941, SS-Gruppenführer Arthur Nebe, commander of Einsatzgruppe B, sent a report to Berlin saying that up until then 45,000 persons had been eliminated. Einsatzgruppe A reported it had already murdered almost all Jews in its area, so it shifted its operations into Belarus to assist B. Einsatzgruppe C, which had begun its killings in western Ukraine to Kharkov and Rostov-on-Don, reported they massacred 3,000 Jews in what was known as the Lvov programme.

All of this killing had a negative psychological effect on some of those tasked with the murders. Himmler made it clear that they would have to simply accept it as policy and cooperate. However, he was aware that a better technique for murdering large numbers of people was needed. One idea was to use Poles, Ukrainians, Balts and Jews, who were already destined to be killed. This was found to be a better solution.

In August 1941, near Minsk, Himmler witnessed a mass killing and nearly fainted during the spectacle. He commented that the execution was not humane and effects on the troops would lower morale. He declared that he wanted a different method of killing. Dr Albert Wildmann of the RSHA's Criminal Technical Institute:

> After only a brief period, the commandos of the Einsatzgruppen got into considerable difficulties. The members of the Einsatz – and special commandos, some of whom were themselves fathers – were in the long run not up to the mental strain caused by the mass shootings, particularly when women and children were involved. There were disputes, refusals to obey orders, drunken orgies, but also serious psychological illness. Himmler, who was at first not aware of the situation was looking for a way of reducing the nervous psychological strain on the men involved in the shooting. From this, in discussions with Heydrich and other leading figures, the plan emerged of using gas vans for this purpose, for the liquidation of women and children in particular ... In September or October 1941, the head of Department IID in the RSHA, SS Obersturmbannführer Rauff was ordered by Heydrich to build gas vans.

The Einsatzgruppen were the first to kill using gas. A special vehicle was built to resemble an ambulance or refrigerator truck and to be airtight. The victims would be shut in the cabin and carbon monoxide was piped in. The first gas van was tested on Russian prisoners in Sachsenhausen concentration camp in autumn 1941. It enabled personnel to murder without looking into the eyes of their victims.

By early 1942, government policy towards the Jews began to change. Following the Wannsee Conference, it was agreed that the Jews would be eradicated, but there would be more structured procedures put in place. Some would be worked to death in concentration camps, the rest would be killed in special extermination camps. This would become the primary method of mass killing, and effectively replaced the Einsatzgruppen campaign of murder in the East The Einsatzgruppen would however remain active in anti-partisan actions, particularly in the Baltic States.

On 22 June 1941, 3 million troops of the German army rolled across the Soviet frontier to begin their conquest of Russia. In this photo soldiers are preparing an 8.8cm Flak gun for a fire mission.

Soldiers on the march along a road with their rifles slung over their shoulders.

(**Opposite, above**) More than likely a motorcycle reconnaissance troop pose for the camera with their sidecar combinations next to a road.

(**Opposite, below**) Soldiers from the Das Reich Division pose for the camera in front of what appears to be a bus being used for troop transportation. Das Reich fought with Army Group Centre and took part in the battle of Yelnya near Smolensk. Einsatzgruppe B was also attached to the rear echelons of Army Group Centre, which saw SS and regular soldiers assisting Einsatzkommando 9 in and around Smolensk, rounding up Jews and other people they regarded as hostile elements, and murdering them.

(**Above**) Soldiers of the SS Totenkopf Division. The Totenkopf Division advanced with Army Group North and took part in the advance through Lithuania and Latvia. Following the drive in Army Group North was Einsatzgruppe A.

The first of eight photographs showing Russian soldiers captured during the German army's advance through the Soviet Union. Millions of Red Army PoWs were rounded up, many being executed in the field by German forces or handed over to the SS and Einsatzgruppen to be shot, under what was known as the Commissar Order. Most, however, died during death marches from the front lines or under inhumane conditions in German PoW and concentration camps.

A photograph of Field Marshal Walter Karl Ernst August von Reichenau. Reichenau was an anti-Semite who equated Jewry with Bolshevism. During the invasion of the Soviet Union he gave approval for the Einsatzgruppen to assist his Wehrmacht units in identifying and registering all Jews in the occupied areas and murdering them.

A soldier, more than likely a motorcycle dispatch rider, has been conversing with Russian locals in a village. The Russian population were often subjected to interrogation. Information gathered was relayed back to SS and police commands. Einsatzgruppen would then move in and round up the Jews, frequently killing them.

Peasant men, women and children are forced to pose for the camera during a cleansing operation.

A local police unit assisting Einsatzgruppen operations during a cleansing action in the rear areas can be seen in this tragic photograph. A peasant mother and her child are executed at the side of a pit.

A member from the German security service or SD reads out a list of crimes committed by the arrested men and women who stand in file prior to their execution.

Suspected insurgents have been rounded up and led away under the supervision of local police to an execution pit.

(**Above**) Three bewildered and frightened men are photographed standing in a grave they have just been forced to dig for themselves. Surrounding them, armed with rifles, stand members of the Einsatzgruppen.

(**Opposite, above**) Wehrmacht soldiers operating in the rear areas along with local police units and Einsatzgruppen converse with local peasant people. Communication with the local populace was often fundamentally key for German units to weed out insurgents in the area or Jews hiding in the surrounding forests and woods. Local folk were regularly given rewards for information. However, giving information was done more out of fear for reprisals.

(**Opposite, below**) Intrigued Wehrmacht soldiers, some with their cameras, observe the hanging of a number of suspected partisans by local police units.

(**Above**) A typical Einsatzgruppen execution. Here troops armed with rifles point their weapons at innocent civilians, half stripped of their clothes, while they stand with their backs to the firing squad.

(**Opposite, above**) Partisans have been rounded up by an army unit and await their fate. Often partisans were publicly hanged as examples, but it was often quicker just to shoot them.

(**Opposite, below**) A female partisan is publicly hanged in the city of Minsk as a deterrent and to pacify the local population. An unidentified German unit can be seen standing around.

Jews forced to dig their own graves in Zboriv, Ukraine, on 5 July 1941.

An Einsatzgruppe firing squad during a partisan liquidation action in the summer of 1941.

A young boy can be seen standing next to his murdered family following an Einsatzgruppe liquidation action on his town in summer 1941.

An unidentified Einsatzgruppe unit execute Soviet civilians kneeling by the side of a mass grave. *(NARA)*

Men of the Ukrainische Hilfspolizei, or Ukrainian Auxiliary Police, which was the official title of the local police formation set up by the Reichskommissariat Ukraine. These mobile police units, which were organized at battalion level, were widely engaged in the murder of Jews and 'pacification' actions in the Ukraine combating partisans. Subordinated to the German Order Police, these police units were responsible for assisting the Einsatzgruppen in various massacres.

Men from a local Order Police unit surround an old Jewish gentlemen, interrogate him and ask for his identity papers. It is probable this photograph was taken during a liquidation action in a town somewhere in western Russia during the summer of 1941.

Russian civilians are executed standing inside a mass grave by an Einsatzgruppe unit in the summer of 1941.

A group of Wehrmacht soldiers smile for the camera during operations in the rear area with police units and Einsatzgruppen.

SS-Obersturmbannführer Emanuel Schäfer. Schäfer commanded Einsatzgruppe II through Poland in 1939. He was an obstinate and cruel individual and later took over security in Serbia where he murdered thousands of Jews.

Two photographs showing the Ordnungspolizei or Order Police interrogating and arresting local people. The Order Police battalions were formed into independent regiments or were attached to Wehrmacht security divisions and Einsatzgruppen. Across the rear areas these police units perpetrated mass murder and were responsible for widespread crimes against humanity and genocide, often solely targeting the civilian population.

(**Above**) A group of female Jews half stripped of their clothes stand next to a mass grave before their execution by an Einsatzgruppe.

(**Opposite, above**) This photograph shows members of the community from the Mizocz ghetto undressing. Mizocz ghetto had initially held some 1,700 Jews. On 13 October 1942, the eve of the ghetto's liquidation, some of the inhabitants rose up against the Germans and were defeated after a short battle. The remaining members of the community were transported from the ghetto to a ravine in the Sdolbunov, south of Rovno. At the edge of the ravine the Jews, mostly women and children, were ordered to undress and then were herded down the ravine and executed. (*USHMM, Instytut Pamieci Narodowej*)

(**Opposite, below**) In this second photograph from the Mizocz ghetto massacre, Jewish women are led naked, some holding infants, and wait in a line before their execution. These frightened and bewildered women were part of a liquidation action by the German gendarmerie and a Ukrainian 'security' team. (*USHMM, Instytut Pamieci Narodowej*)

(**Opposite, above**) In this third photograph, a German policeman prepares to complete a mass execution of the remaining inhabitants of the Mizocz ghetto by shooting two Jewish children, who can still be seen sitting up looking very distressed. (*USHMM Instytut Pamieci Narodowej*)

(**Opposite, below**) In this fourth photograph, the German policeman is seen shooting the remaining inhabitants of the Mizocz ghetto that are still showing signs of life. Note the young child still sitting upright, obviously terrified at the whole spectacle. (*USHMM Instytut Pamieci Narodowej*)

(**Above**) German police and auxiliaries in civilian clothes look on as a group of Jewish women are forced to undress before their execution. (*USHMM Instytut Pamieci Narodowej*)

Chapter Three

Murder in the Baltic States

General Ritter von Leeb's two-pronged offensive along the Baltic opened up at first light on the morning of 22 June 1941. His force, consisting of 16th and 18th Armies, smashed through the Soviet defences. Russian soldiers stood helpless in its path, too shocked to take action. Over the weeks to come, troops of German Army Group North continued to chew through enemy positions heading through Lithuania, Latvia and Estonia, towards their objective – Leningrad. In their wake was Einsatzgruppe A. It entered Kaunas and began a pogrom. By 27 June, with the assistance of some criminals released from the prison and some anti-Semitic groups, some 4,000 Jews were killed, either in the streets or they were escorted to nearby pits and ditches and massacred.

In early July the Einsatzgruppe A sent a radio communication to its command centre with a progress report, with many of them already entering Latvia:

> Einsatzkommando 1a: Location July 3, 1941: Under way from Mitau to Riga (comunication by radiogram)
> Einsatzkommando 1b: Location Kaunas
> Einsatzkommando 2: Location July 3, 1941: Siauliai, NKVD Building.
> Siauliai: 35,000 inhabitants (12–15,000 Jews). About 2,000 Jews are still left. The others have fled. The prison is empty. In order to keep the war plants and the plants vital for the population operational, the Wehrmacht is, for the time being, not in a position to dispose of the Jewish manpower still available and fit for work.

On 1 July, Einsatzgruppe A commander SS-Brigadeführer Dr Franz Walter Stahlecker appointed the Nazi collaborator Victors Arajs to lead a Latvian Auxiliary Security Police Sonderkommando of 300 men, known as the 'Arajs Kommando'. The group was composed of students and former anti-Semitic right-wing officers, all of whom were volunteers and free to leave at any time. The next day, under the direction of the Einsatzgruppen, they began their own pogrom in Riga, consisting of the murder of Jews, Roma and mental patients. Between 5 and 7 July they burned down the city's Choral Synagogue and killed 2,200 Jews. They then went on to participate in various massacres of civilians along the eastern borders of the Soviet Union.

Assisting these atrocities, local auxiliary police known as the Hilfspolizei or help police, and various local officials, played roles in rounding up and massacring Jewish Lithuanians, Latvians, and Estonians. They helped the Einsatzgruppen and other killing units to locate Jews, and they also increasingly assisted in massacres of Jews along with the Arajs Kommandos, due to the immense task the Einsatzgruppen were faced with. On 15 October 1941, Einsatzgruppe A sent a positive report of its action:

<u>Reich Secret Document</u>

Einsatzgruppe A

General Report up to 15 October 1941

Cleansing [of Jews] and securing the area of operation.

Encouragement of Self-cleansing Aktionen (Selbstreinigungs-aktionen)

Basing [oneself] on the consideration that the population of the Baltic countries had suffered most severely under the rule of Bolshevism and Jewry while they were incorporated into the U.S.S.R., it was to be expected that after liberation from this foreign rule they would themselves to a large extent eliminate those of the enemy left behind after the retreat of the Red Army. It was the task of the Security Police to set these self-cleansing movements going and to direct them into the right channels in order to achieve the aim of this cleansing as rapidly as possible. It was no less important to establish as unshakable and provable facts for the future that it was the liberated population itself which took the most severe measures, on its own initiative, against the Bolshevik and Jewish enemy, without any German instructions being evident.

In Lithuania this was achieved for the first time by activating the partisans in Kovno. To our surprise it was not easy at first to set any large-scale anti-Jewish pogrom in motion there. Klimatis, the leader of the partisan group referred to above, who was the first to be recruited for this purpose, succeeded in starting a pogrom with the aid of instructions given him by a small advance detachment operating in Kovno, in such a way that no German orders or instructions could be observed by outsiders. In the course of the first pogrom during the night of June 25/26, the Lithuanian partisans eliminated more than 1,500 Jews, set fire to several synagogues or destroyed them by other means, and burned down an area consisting of about sixty houses inhabited by Jews. During the nights that followed, 2,300 Jews were eliminated in the same way. In other parts of Lithuania similar Aktionen followed the example set in Kovno, but on a smaller scale, and including some Communists who had been left behind.

These self-cleansing Aktionen ran smoothly because the Wehrmacht authorities who had been informed showed understanding for this procedure. At the same time it was obvious from the beginning that only the first days after the

Occupation would offer the opportunity for carrying out pogroms. After the disarmament of the partisans the self-cleansing Aktionen necessarily ceased.

It proved to be considerably more difficult to set in motion similar cleansing Aktionen and pogroms in Latvia. The main reason was that the entire national leadership, especially in Riga, had been killed or deported by the Soviets. Even in Riga it proved possible by means of appropriate suggestions to the Latvian auxiliary police to get an anti-Jewish pogrom going, in the course of which all the synagogues were destroyed and about 400 Jews killed. As the population on the whole has been pacified very quickly in Riga, it was not possible to arrange further pogroms.

Both in Kovno and in Riga evidence was taken on film and by photographs to establish, as far as possible, that the first spontaneous executions of Jews and Communists were carried out by Lithuanians and Latvians.

In Estonia there was no opportunity of instigating pogroms owing to the relatively small number of Jews. The Estonian self-defence units only eliminated some individual Communists, who were particularly hated, but in general limited themselves to carrying out arrests.

The Fight against Jewry

It was to be expected from the beginning that the Jewish problem in the Ostland could not be solved by pogroms alone. At the same time the Security Police had basic, general orders for cleansing operations aimed at a maximum elimination of the Jews. Large-scale executions were therefore carried out in the cities and the countryside by Sonderkommandos, which were assisted by selected units – partisan groups in Lithuania, and parties of the Latvian Auxiliary Police in Latvia. The work of the execution units was carried out smoothly. Where Lithuanian and Latvian forces were attached to the execution units, the first to be chosen were those who had had members of their families and relatives killed or deported by the Russians.

Particularly severe and extensive measures became necessary in Lithuania. In some places – especially in Kovno – the Jews had armed themselves and took an active part in sniping and arson. In addition, the Jews of Lithuania cooperated most closely with the Soviets.

The total number of Jews liquidated in Lithuania is 71,105.

During the pogrom 3,800 Jews were eliminated in Kovno and about 1,200 in the smaller cities.

In Latvia too, Jews took part in acts of sabotage and arson after the entry of the German Wehrmacht. In Duenaburg so many fires were started by Jews that a large part of the city was destroyed. The electric power station was burned out completely. Streets inhabited mainly by Jews remained untouched.

Up to now 30,000 Jews have been executed in Latvia. The pogrom in Riga eliminated 500.

Most of the 4,500 Jews living in Estonia at the start of the Eastern campaign fled with the retreating Red Army. About 2,000 stayed behind. In Reval there were about 1,000 Jews.

The arrest of all male Jews over the age of sixteen is almost completed. With the exception of the doctors and the Jewish Elders appointed by the Sonderkommando, they are being executed by the Estonian self-defence under the supervision of Sonderkommando.

Jewesses between the ages of 16 and 60 in Reval and Pernau who are fit for work were arrested and used to cut peat and for other work.

At present a camp is being built at Harku, to which all the Jews in Estonia will be sent, so that in a short time Estonia will be cleared of Jews.

After the carrying out of the first large-scale executions in Lithuania and Latvia it already proved that the total elimination of the Jews is not possible there, at least not at the present time. As a large part of the skilled trades is in Jewish hands in Lithuania and Latvia, and some (glaziers, plumbers, stove-builders, shoe-makers) are almost entirely Jewish, a large proportion of Jewish craftsmen are indispensable at present for the repair of essential installations, for the reconstruction of destroyed cities, and for work of military importance. Although the employers aim at replacing Jewish labour with Lithuanian or Latvian workers, it is not yet possible to replace all the Jews presently employed, particularly in the larger cities. In cooperation with the labour exchange offices, however, Jews who are no longer fit for work are picked up and will be executed shortly in small Aktionen.

It must also be noted in this connection that in some places there has been considerable resistance by offices of the Civil Administration against large-scale executions. This was confronted in every case by pointing out that it was a matter of carrying out orders [involving] a basic principle.

Apart from organizing and carrying out the executions, preparations were begun from the first days of the operation for the establishment of ghettos in the larger cities. This was particularly urgent in Kovno, where there were 30,000 Jews in a total population of 152,400. At the end of the early pogroms therefore, a Jewish Committee was summoned and informed that the German authorities had so far seen no reason to interfere in the conflicts between the Lithuanians and the Jews. A condition for the creation of a normal situation would be, first of all, the creation of a Jewish ghetto. When the Jewish Committee remonstrated, it was explained that there was no other possibility of preventing further pogroms. At this the Jews at once declared that they were ready to do everything to transfer their co-racial as quickly as possible to the

Viliampole Quarter, where it was planned to establish the Jewish ghetto. This area is situated in the triangle between the River Memel and a branch of the river, and is linked with Kovno by only one bridge, and easily sealed off.

In spite of the optimistic reports, by November Himmler was becoming increasingly disgruntled by the slow pace of exterminations in the Baltic States. The Reichsführer wanted to transport Jews from Germany to Riga. To this end he decided to liquidate the Riga ghetto which consisted of some 35,000 Jews. SS-Obergruppenführer Friedrich Jeckeln was assigned the task. He had already excelled in the SS as one of the key perpetrators of the Babi Yar massacre. Now he planned to murder all the inhabitants of the ghetto.

The first phase began with the victims being told that they were being relocated and advised to bring up to 20kg of possessions with them. They were then assembled and moved in columns of a thousand towards the specially prepared execution pits that were dug by 300 Russian PoWs in the nearby forest of Rumbula. Some 1,700 men, including 300 members of the Arajs Kommando, accompanied the Jews to the forest.

Once the victims arrived in the forest they were asked to undress and deposit their valuables in designated locations and collection boxes. They were then marched towards the murder pits naked. The killers carefully watched the frightened victims undressing in case some resisted and caused panic. If there were too many people arriving near the killing area, they were held back in nearby woods until their turn came.

On 30 November and 8 and 9 December thousands of victims were led down the ramps into the pits in single file, ten at a time. Two hundred were shot per hour. Some 27,500 Latvian Jews were murdered in these pre-dug pits. About 1,000 were killed in the streets of the city on their way to the execution site. About 4,500 skilled Jewish male workers and about 500 Jewish women who had been classified as seamstresses survived the Rumbula massacres. Around 1,500 able-bodied Jews were spared execution so they could be used for slave labour in the nearby ghetto. As for Jeckeln, he was promoted to Leader of the SS Upper Section, Ostland.

On 1 December 1941, Kommando 3 of Einsatzgruppe A sent a summary report from their area:

Final Summary of executions carried out in the operating area of EK [Einsatzkommando] 3 up to 1 December 1941.

I can confirm today that Einsatzkommando 3 has achieved the goal of solving the Jewish problem in Lithuania. There are no more Jews in Lithuania, apart from working Jews and their families. These number: in Shavli, about 4,500; in Kovno, about 15,000; and in Vilna, about 15,000.

I wanted to eliminate the working Jews and their families as well, but the Civil Administration (Reichskommissar) and the Wehrmacht attacked me most sharply and issued a prohibition against having these Jews and their families shot.

The goal of clearing Lithuania of Jews could only be achieved through the establishment of a specially selected Mobile Commando under the command of SS Obersturmführer Hamann, who adopted my aims fully and ensured the cooperation of the Lithuanian Partisans and the Civil Authorities concerned.

The carrying-out of such Aktionen is first of all an organizational problem. The decision to clear each sub-district systematically of Jews called for a thorough preparation for each Aktion and the study of local conditions. The Jews had to be concentrated in one or more localities and, in accordance with their numbers, a site had to be selected and pits dug. The marching distance from the concentration points to the pits averaged 4 to 5 kms. The Jews were brought to the place of execution in groups of 500, with at least 2 kms. distance between groups ... All the officers and men of my command in Kovno took active part in the Grossaktionen in Kovno. Only one official of the intelligence corps was released from participation on account of illness.

I consider the Aktionen against the Jews of EK 3 to be virtually completed. The remaining working Jews and Jewesses are urgently needed, and I can imagine that this manpower will continue to be needed urgently after the winter has ended. I am of the opinion that the male working Jews should be sterilized immediately to prevent reproduction. Should any Jewesses nevertheless become pregnant, she is to be liquidated.

(signed) Jäger
SS Standartenführer

By late 1941 the Einsatzkommandos settled into their new headquarters in Riga, Kovno, and the Estonian capital Tallinn. In Estonia most of the Jews had fled across into the Soviet Union, and virtually all of those who remained, some 1,000, had been killed by Einsatzgruppe A and local collaborators before the end of 1941. The Roma people were also killed or put to work as slave labourers. Thousands of ethnic Estonians and Russians who were accused of being communist sympathisers or the relatives of communist sympathisers were massacred.

With the occupation of the Baltic States complete, Einsatzgruppe A grew less mobile, relying increasingly on the Arajs Kommando and similar groups to kill remaining Jews, communist sympathisers and disabled people in the area.

The advance by Einsatzgruppe A through the Baltic States had been swift and barbaric. A total of 137,346 people had been murdered by Einsatzkommando 3 alone. This was only part of Einsatzgruppe A. Between Einsatzkommandos 1, 1a, 1b, 1c and 2 there were some 200,000 more.

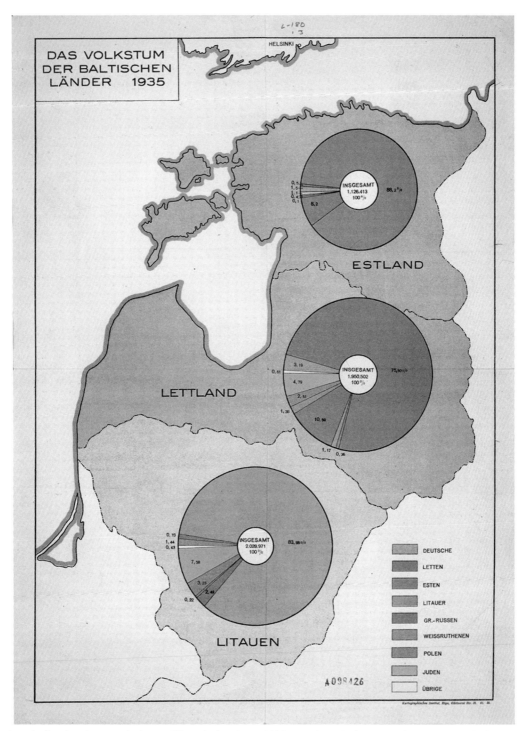

A pie chart indicating the populations of Estonia, Latvia and Lithuania by ethnic group, that accompanied the report of SS-Brigadier General Stahlecker to the Reich Security Main Office, Berlin. This chart, entitled 'The Population of the Baltic States 1935', shows that in 1935, 7.58% of Lithuanians were Jews. In 1939 the proportion of Jews increased to nearly 10% after the contested Vilna region was returned to Lithuania. (NARA)

Two photographs showing German troops resting during their attack through the Baltic States. These soldiers were part of Army Group North advancing through Lithuania, Latvia and Estonia, towards their objective – Leningrad.

Soldiers enter a Latvian town during their advance through the country. In their wake were units of Einsatzgruppe A.

As the German army advanced through the Baltic States, Jews started fleeing east. However, many were unable to go east and went into hiding. As a result thousands were captured by police units. In this photograph, Lithuania Jews are seen digging pits in the Kuziai Forest before they were all murdered. This massacre took place near the village of Dvariukai. Fifty-seven men were taken out of their homes and led to Siauliai and kept in the local prison. Thirty were chosen to dig pits in the forest, which were later used as the mass graves for the Jews of Siauliai. The remaining twenty-seven men, who were not taken to work, were shot on 10 July 1941.

(**Above**) A group of Wehrmacht soldiers during a lull in a partisan operation. Himmler had forbidden photographs of any of the death squad murders. However, it was common for both the men of the Einsatzgruppen and some infantry to take pictures to send to their loved ones. It is suggested widespread approval of the massacres by the Einsatzgruppen, German army and SS.

(**Opposite, above**) Einsatzgruppen soldiers are seen shooting Jews in a ditch. These mobile killing units often acted swiftly, taking the Jewish population by complete surprise. Units entered a town or city and rounded up all Jewish men, women, and children, and regularly took away many Communist party leaders and gypsies. Members of the Einsatzgruppen, frequently assisted by local police, Order Police units and Wehrmacht security units, marched their victims to open fields, forests and ravines on the outskirts of the cleansed towns and cities where they would murder them in huge, open pits.

(**Opposite, below**) A member of an Einsatzkommando ensures that the civilians he has just shot show no signs of life. He can be seen pointing a gun at one of the victims he thinks maybe still alive.

A Latvian policeman walks along a mass grave.

Jewish people arrested by local Lithuanian forces in July 1941 have been tied together with rope and prepared to be led away for execution.

On 7 July 1941, a Lithuanian militia unit force a group of Jewish women from the Panevezys ghetto to undress before their execution in the Pajuoste Forest. This soldier more than likely belongs to an auxiliary company of the Union of Lithuanian Riflemen, which was used in shooting actions from the very beginning of the German occupation of Lithuania. This auxiliary company assisted Einsatzkommando 3 during in its cleansing operations throughout Lithuania. The entire population of the ghetto, approximately 7,523 Jews, were brought to the Pajuoste Forest and killed.

Two photographs showing Jewish prisoners being escorted by a Lithuanian policeman. On 26 June 1941, the Wehrmacht entered Vilna, followed by the Einsatzgruppen B. Local Lithuanian leaders advocated ethnic cleansing of Jews and Poles and, throughout the summer, German troops and their Lithuanian collaborators killed more than 21,000 Jews living in Vilnius in a mass extermination programme.

Jewish men are forced to the edge of a pit prior to their execution by local police and Einsatzkommandos.

Chapter Four

Last Years

By late 1941 it was determined that the Einsatzgruppen alone would be unable to kill the entire Jewish population of Russia, despite help from native auxiliaries, police and the Waffen-SS. In December 1941 a second operation began: ghettoization of the Jews. The experience in Poland had shown that containing Jews in ghettos was successful. By the end of 1941 some 3.5 million Polish Jews were living in ghettos. But it was a stop-gap solution – a temporary measure while the Nazi leadership deliberated on how to dispose of the Jews once and for all.

With ghettoization as policy across Europe, massacres were reduced. But then, with the liquidation of the ghettos, the German Reserve Police Battalion together with members of the Jewish Police, the Sonderdienst battalion of Ukrainian Trawnikis, SS soldiers and Einsatzgruppen, the Jews were rounded up and sent to death camps. Some were marched into nearby woods where Einsatzgruppen murdered them.

By the summer of 1942, the Einsatzgruppen were employed only in supporting anti-partisan operations and assisting in the liquidation of the ghettos.

By the early winter of 1943, as military events beset the German war machine on the Eastern Front, Himmler, concerned that Germany could lose the war, ordered the formation of a special task force known as Sonderkommando 1005, under SS-Standartenführer Paul Blobel. The unit had initially been put together purely to conceal evidence of the genocide at the Reinhard murder camps of Treblinka, Belzec and Sobibor. Now however the units, known as Leichenkommandos, or corpse units, were given the task of exhuming bodies in mass graves and burning them.

As the war dragged on into 1944, there was a dull conviction by the Germans that the war was lost. In the summer the Soviets were pushing the Wehrmacht, Waffen-SS and the remnants of the Einsatzgruppen further west into Poland, expelling them from Russian soil forever. By now the bulk of the Einsatzgruppe personnel had been absorbed into the various Waffen-SS combat units or been transferred to the numerous death camps that were completing their operations.

The Einsatzgruppen would no longer play a major role in the holocaust, but they had achieved all that was required of them. By the end of the war many of the soldiers who had served in the Einsatzgruppen had been killed in action. However, of those that survived, most never faced justice and simply returned to civilian life.

Four photographs showing Waffen-SS troops preparing for a liquidation action in Russia in the summer of 1943. Both SS and regular troops assisted local police units and auxiliaries to round up remaining Jewish communities, and either have them murdered in nearby forests or ravines, or sent to labour or death camps.

Two photographs showing the deportation action of Jewish men, women and children. Often during these actions these hapless people were not transported from their ghettos, but to nearby forests or woods and systematically killed by firing squad.

An Einsatzkommando firing squad are seen during the murder of some of the Jewish community from Bochnia in Poland. It is estimated that approximately 15,000 Jews were deported from Bochnia, with at least a further 1,800 killed in the town and its surrounding forests.

SS-Reichsführer Heinrich Himmler seen during a parade inspecting members of a Wehrmacht security unit.

Epilogue

It is estimated that between 1939 and 1945 the Einsatzgruppen and related murder squads had killed at least 2 million people, including 1.3 million Jews.

On 10 September 1947 the US Military Government for Germany created the Military Tribunal II-A (later renamed Tribunal II) to try the Einsatzgruppen case to be tried at Nuremburg. The twenty-four defendants were all leaders of the mobile security and killing units of the SS, the Einsatzgruppen. On 29 July 1947 the defendants were indicted on three counts of criminality: crimes against humanity, war crimes, and membership of organizations declared criminal by the International Military Tribunal. Each defendant was charged with all three counts, between the period of their activity from May 1941 to July 1943.

Map from the Stahlecker Report entitled 'Jewish Executions Carried out by Einsatzgruppe A', showing coffins and numbers of executions carried out in Europe. This map was entered into evidence at the Einsatzgruppen trial. It shows the area between the German-Soviet Demarcation Line and the area of the furthest German army advance in the Soviet Union at the time. A summary report of charts, maps, and illustrations was compiled by SS-Brigadier General Stahlecker. The information was presented to the Reich Security Main Office in Berlin in February 1942. The deaths recorded in this map occurred between 16 October 1941 and 30 January 1942.
(USHMM, Thomas Wartenberg)

At last Otto Ohlendorf, Heinz Jost, Erich Naumann, Otto Rasch, Erwin Schulz, Franz Six and Paul Blobel received retribution for all those that perished at their hands. Fourteen death sentences and two life sentences were among the judgments handed out. Of these, only four executions were carried out on 7 June 1951, the remaining sentences were reduced. Four additional Einsatzgruppe leaders were later tried and executed by other nations.

Soviet officers preside over the opening and exhumation of a mass grave at Fort IX. During the German occupation of the city in the war several of these forts became the sites of mass murder perpetrated by Einsatzkommandos and their Lithuanian collaborators against the Jews of Kovno and Jewish deportees from central and western Europe. In the summer of 1941 Jewish men and women from Kovno were captured by Lithuanian nationalists in random acts of violence and sent to Fort VII where they were raped and/or murdered. In July alone over 3,000 were killed at this fort. At least 200 more were murdered at Fort V and 500 at Fort IV in this period. The anti-Jewish violence became more systematic after the German Einsatzkommando III, led by SS-Standartenführer Karl Jäger, asserted control over the area toward the end of the summer. (*USHMM, George Kadish/Zvi Kadushin*)

View of Fort IX after the liberation. (*USHMM, George Kadish/Zvi Kadushin*)

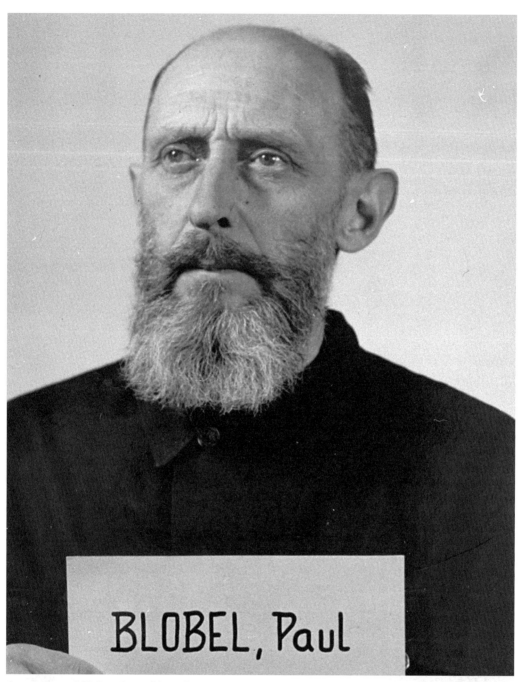

BLOBEL, Paul

A mugshot of SS-Standartenführer Paul Blobel. Blobel participated in the massacres at Babi Yar and Kharkov. In January 1942 he was relieved of duty for health reasons related to his excessive drinking. Subsequently he was put in charge of Aktion 1005, the operation to obliterate the traces of the mass murders committed by the Germans by disinterring and cremating the bodies from the mass graves in the German-occupied Soviet Union. Blobel was tried and convicted at the Einsatzgruppen Trial and sentenced to death. He was hanged at Landsberg prison on 8 June 1951. (NARA)

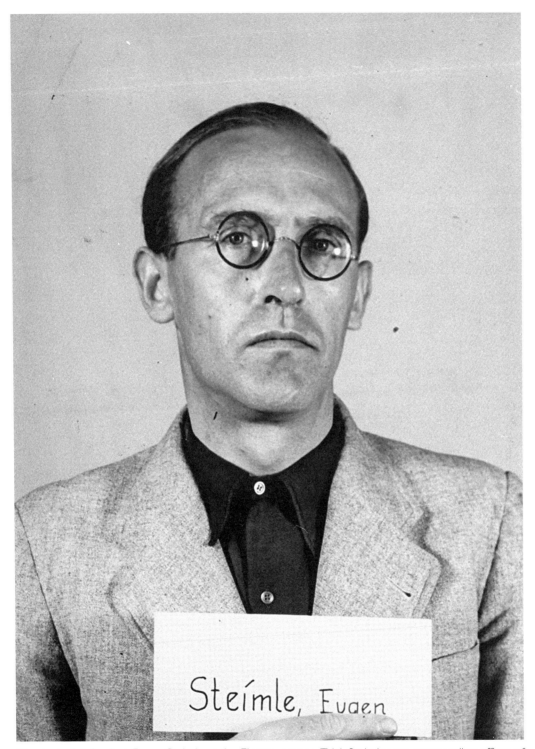

Mugshot of defendant Eugen Steimle at the Einsatzgruppen Trial. Steimle was commanding officer of Sonderkommando 7a in Einsatzgruppe B and of Sonderkommando 4a in Einsatzgruppe C. *(NARA)*

Defendant Franz Six at the Einsatzgruppen Trial. Six was commanding officer of Vorkommando Moscow of Einsatzgruppe B. *(NARA)*

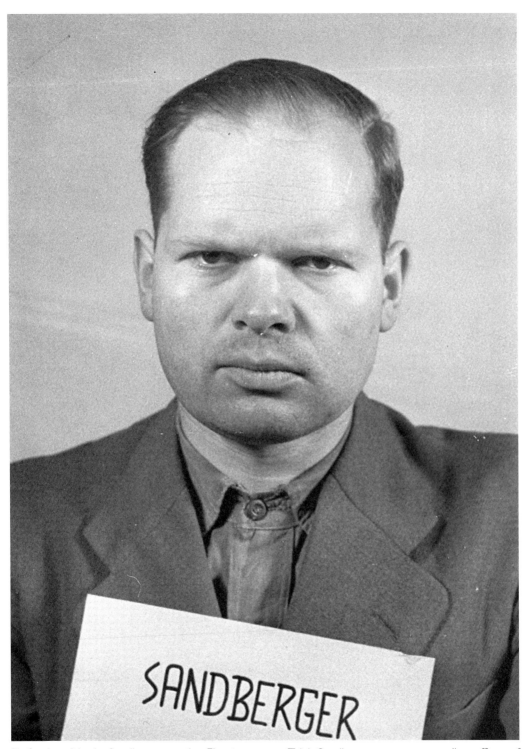

Defendant Martin Sandberger at the Einsatzgruppen Trial. Sandberger was commanding officer of Einsatzkommando 1a of Einsatzgruppe A. (*NARA*)

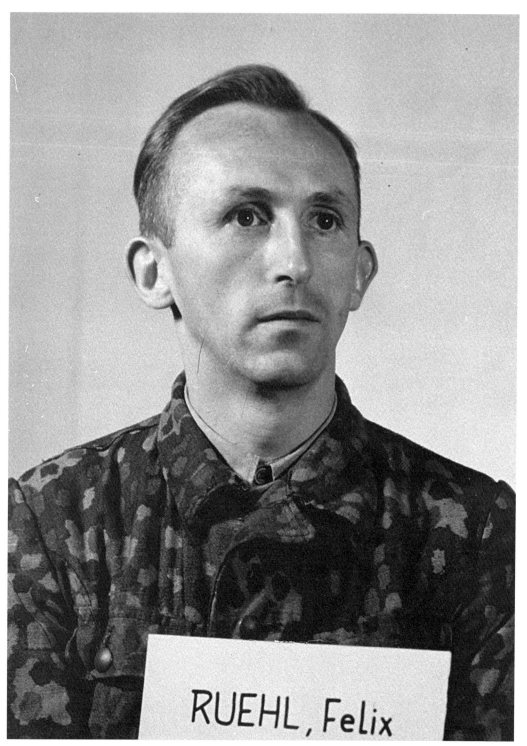

Defendant Felix Ruehl at the Einsatzgruppen Trial. Ruehl was an officer in Sonderkommando 10b of Einsatzgruppe D. (NARA)

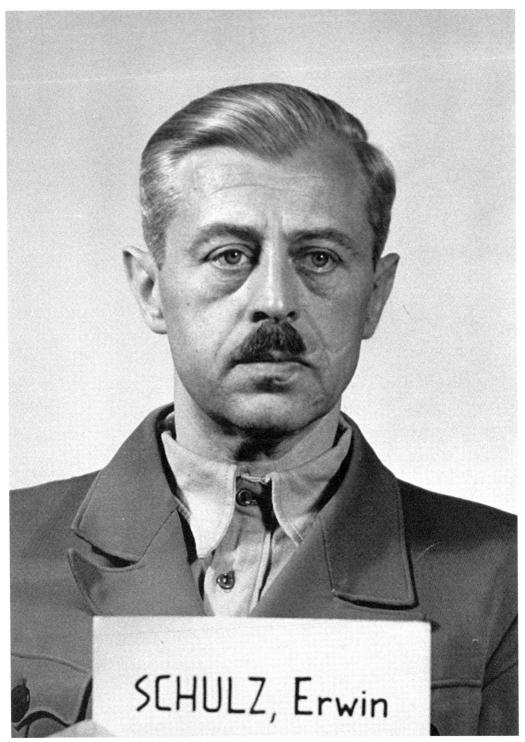

Defendant Erwin Schulz at the Einsatzgruppen Trial. Schulz was commanding officer of Einsatzkommando 5 of Einsatzgruppe C. (NARA)

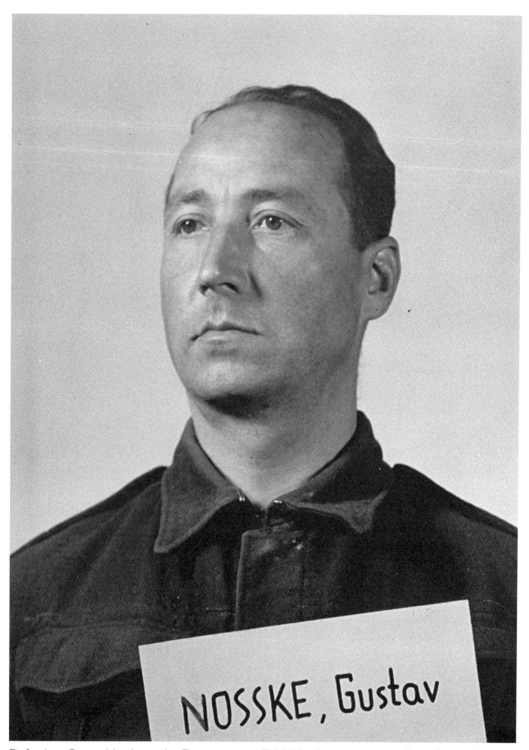

Defendant Gustav Nosske at the Einsatzgruppen Trial. Nosske was commanding officer of Einsatzkommando 12 of Einsatzgruppe D. (*NARA*)

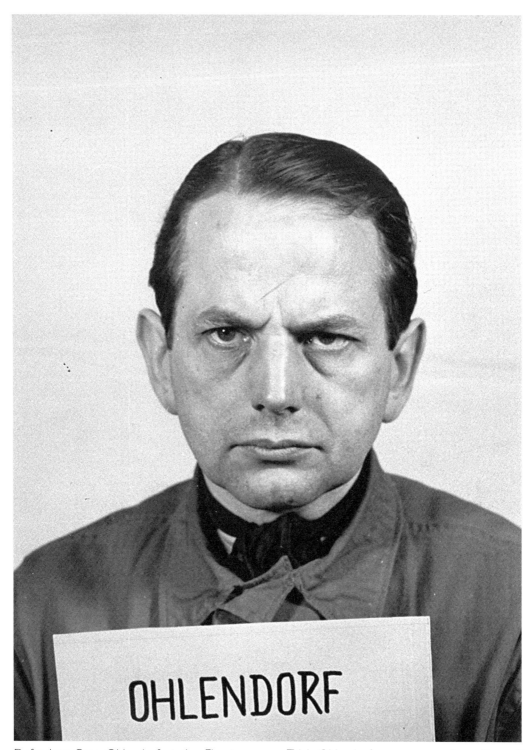

Defendant Otto Ohlendorf at the Einsatzgruppen Trial. Ohlendorf was commanding officer of Einsatzgruppe D. (NARA)

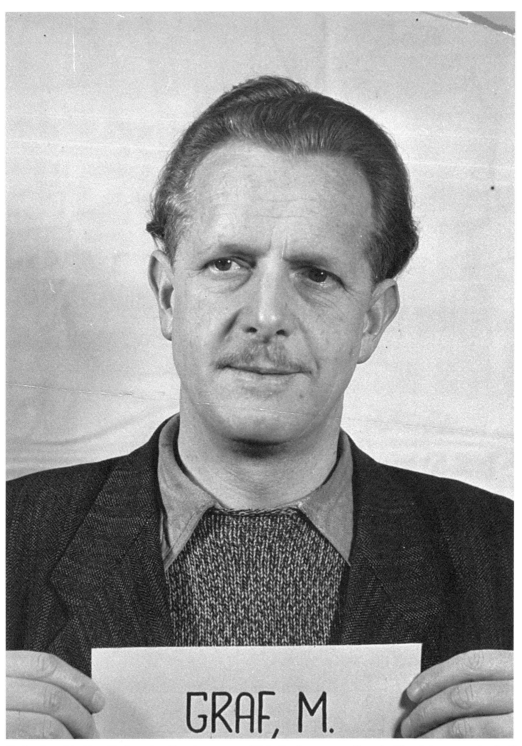

Defendant Mathias Graf at the Einsatzgruppen Trial. Graf was an officer in Einsatzkommando 6 of Einsatzgruppe C. (*NARA*)

Defendant Walter Haensch at the Einsatzgruppen Trial. Haensch was commanding officer of Sonder-kommando 4b of Einsatzgruppe C. (NARA)

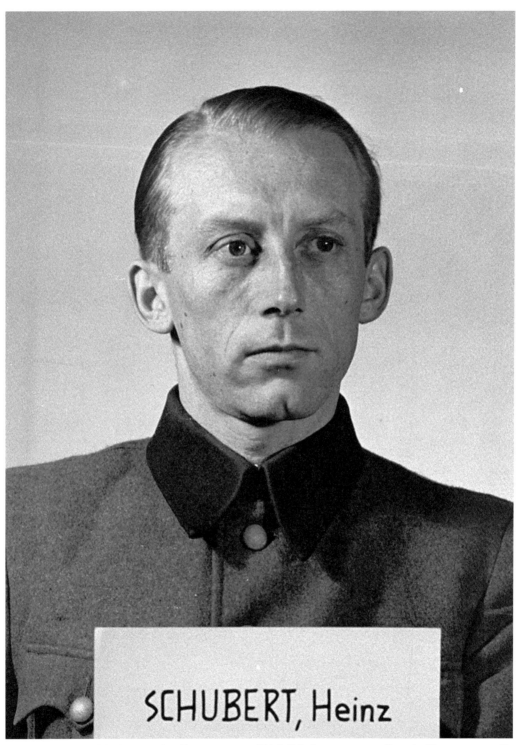

Defendant Heinz Schubert at the Einsatzgruppen Trial. Schubert was an officer in Einsatzgruppe D. (*NARA*)

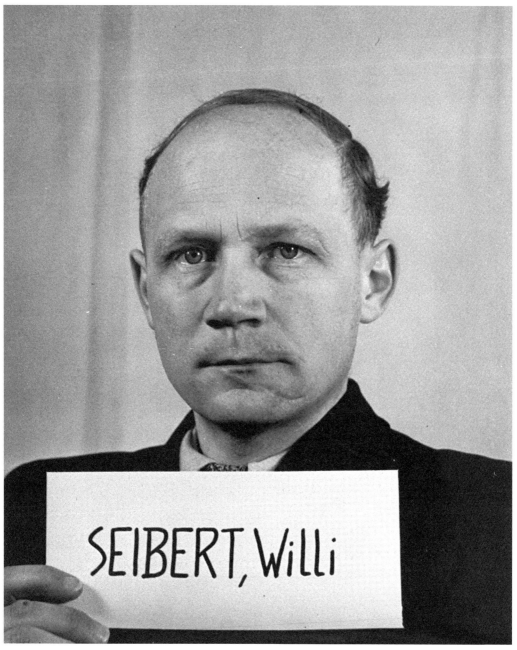

Defendant Willi Seibert at the Einsatzgruppen Trial. Seibert was the Deputy Chief of Einsatzgruppe D. (NARA)

Defendant Erich Naumann at the Einsatzgruppen Trial. Naumann was the commanding officer of Einsatzgruppe B. (NARA)

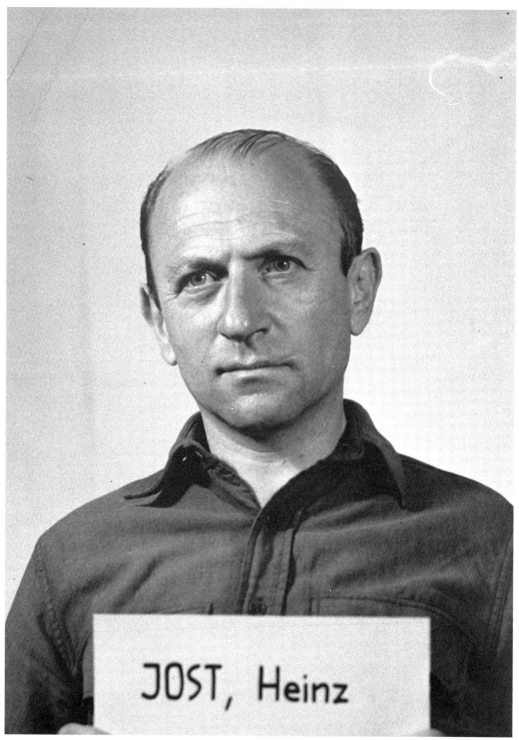

Defendant Heinz Jost at the Einsatzgruppen Trial. Jost was the commanding officer of Einsatzgruppe A. (*NARA*)

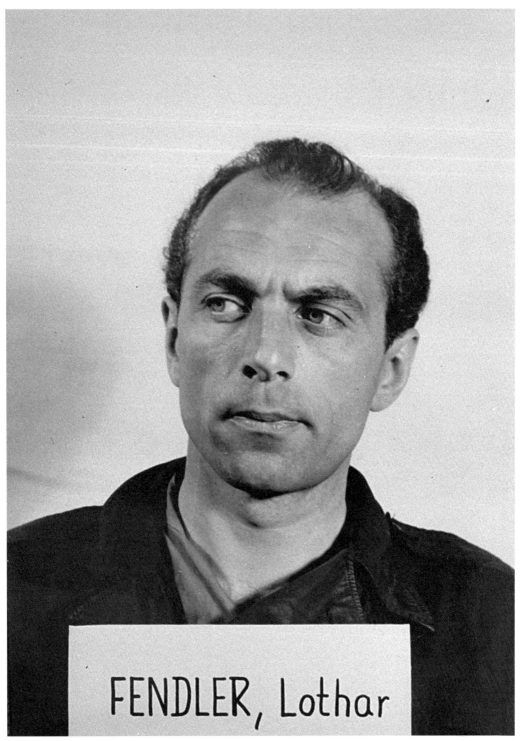

Defendant Lothar Fendler at the Einsatzgruppen Trial. Fendler was deputy chief of Sonderkommando 4b of Einsatzgruppe C. (*NARA*)

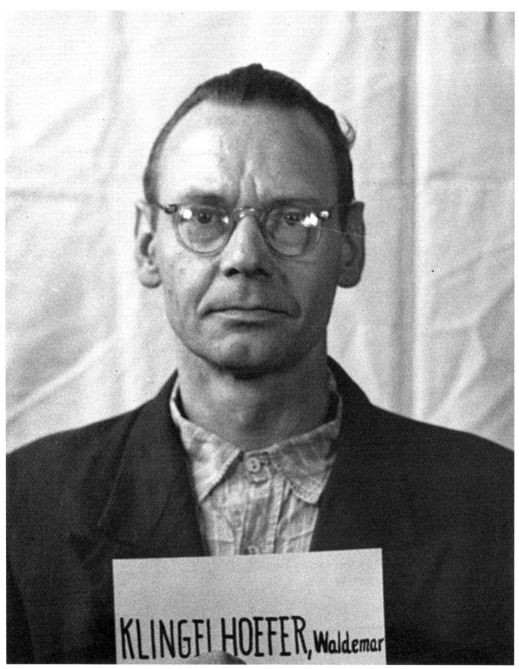

Defendant Waldemar Klingelhoefer at the Einsatzgruppen Trial. Klingelhoefer was a member of Sonderkommando 7b in Einsatzgruppe B, and commanding officer of Vorkommando Moscow. (NARA)

Defendant Emil Haussmann at the Einsatzgruppen Trial. Haussmann was an officer of Einsatzkommando 12 of Einsatzgruppe D. He committed suicide 31 July 1947 before the trial began. (*NARA*)

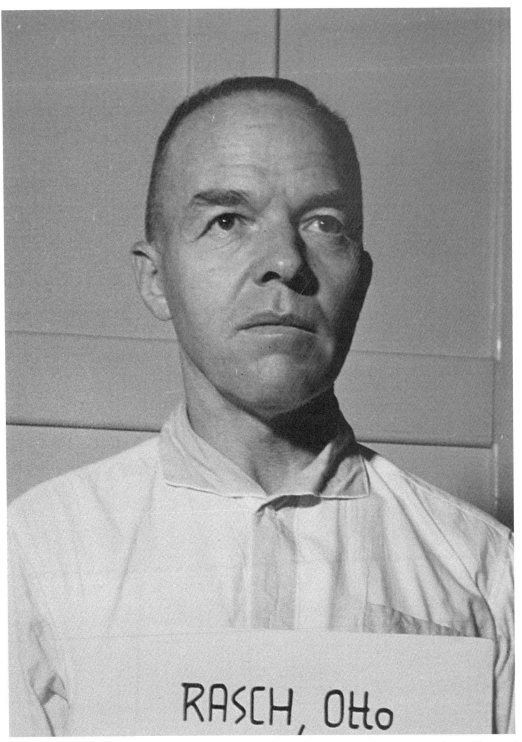

Defendant Otto Rasch at the Einsatzgruppen Trial. Rasch was the commanding officer of Einsatzgruppe C. *(NARA)*

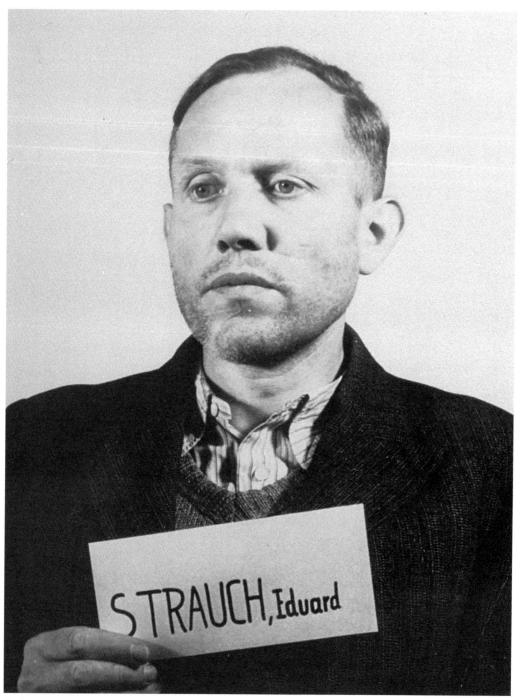

Defendant Eduard Strauch at the Einsatzgruppen Trial. Strauch was the commanding officer of Einsatzkommando 2 of Einsatzgruppe A. *(NARA)*

Structure of the Reich Main Security Office (RSHA)

Amt 1: Personnel and organization

Headed by SS-Gruppenführer Dr Werner Best. Succeeded in 1940 by SS-Brigadeführer Bruno Streckenbach in April 1944. Erich Ehrlinger took over as department chief.

Amt 2: Administration and finance

Headed by SS-Brigadeführer Professor Franz Six.

Amt 3: Internal police intelligence

Headed by SS-Gruppenführer Otto Ohlendorf.

Amt 4: Gestapo

The Secret State Police that operated above the law with unlimited powers of arrest throughout the Reich. Headed by SS-Gruppenführer Heinrich Müller and SS-Obersturmbannführer Adolf Eichmann.

Amt 5 - KRIPO

The criminal police with powers of arrest in ordinary police matters. Originally led by SS-Gruppenführer Arthur Nebe and later by SS-Oberführer Friedrich Panzinger.

Amt 6 – External police intelligence

Operated outside Germany. Originally led by SS-Brigadeführer Heinz Jost and later by SS-Brigadeführer Walter Schellenberg.

Amt 7 – Written records

Overseen by Franz Six and later by SS-Obersturmbannführer Paul Dittel.

Einsatzgruppen operations in Poland, September 1939

For the invasion of Poland there were seven Einsatzgruppen of battalion strength, each subdivided into four Einsatzkommandos of company strength.

Einsatzgruppe I

Operated with the 14th Army in southern Poland.
Commander: SS-Brigadeführer Streckenbach.

Einsatzkommando 1/I: SS-Sturmbannführer Dr Hahn.

Einsatzkommando 2/I: SS-Sturmbannführer Müller.

Einsatzkommando 3/I: SS-Sturmbannführer Dr Hasselberg.

Einsatzkommando 4/I (also known as SS-Bataillon Kreuder):
SS-Sturmbannführer Dr Brunner.

Sonderkommando: Kommandeur Johann Schmer.

Einsatzgruppe II

Operated with the 10th Army in Army Group Centre.
Commander: SS-Obersturmbannführer Schäfer.

Einsatzkommando 1/II: SS-Obersturmbannführer Sens.

Einsatzkommando 2/II: SS-Sturmbannführer Rux.

Einsatzgruppe III

Operated with the 8th Army in Army Group Centre.
Commander: SS-Sturmbannführer Dr Herbert Fischer.

Einsatzkommando 1/III: SS-Sturmbannführer Scharpwinkel.

Einsatzkommando 2/III: SS-Sturmbannführer Dr Liphardt.

Einsatzgruppe IV

Operated with the 4th Army within Army Group North.
Commander: SS-Brigadeführer Lothar Beutel.

Einsatzkommando 1/IV: SS-Sturmbannführer Dr Bischoff.

Einsatzkommando 2/IV: SS-Sturmbannführer Dr Hammer.

Einsatzgruppe V

Operated with the 3rd Army within Army Group North.
Commander: SS-Standartenführer Ernst Damzog.

Einsatzkommando 1/V: SS-Sturmbannführer Dr. Graefe.
Einsatzkommando 2/V: SS-Sturmbannführer Dr. Schefe.
Einsatzgruppe 3/V: SS-Sturmbannführer und Regierungsrat Walter Albath.

Einsatzgruppe VI

Operated in Wielkopolska and the upper regions of Silesia.
Commander: SS-Oberführer Erich Naumann.

Einsatzkommando 1/VI: SS-Sturmbannführer Sommer.
Einsatzkommando 2/VI: SS-Sturmbannführer Flesch.

Einsatzgruppe z.b.V.

Operated in Upper Silesia and Cieszyn Silesia region.
Commanders: SS-Oberführer Dr. Rasch and SS-Obergruppenführer von Woyrsch.

Einsatzkommando 16

Operated in Pomerania.
Commander: SS-Obersturmbannführer Dr Tröger.

Einsatzgruppen task force on the Eastern Front

The list includes Einsatzkommandos, which were sub-groups of the Einsatzgruppen totalling 3,000 men. Einsatzkommandos usually contained 500–1,000 personnel.

Einsatzgruppe A

Attached to Army Group North was formed in Gumbinnen in East Prussia on 23 June 1941. Deployed Lithuanian Border.

Commanders, from 22 June 1941 to 10 October 1944:

SS-Brigadeführer und Generalmajor der Polizei Dr Franz Walter Stahlecker

Brigadeführer und Generalmajor der Polizei Heinz Jost

SS-Oberführer und Oberst der Polizei Dr Humbert Achamer-Pifrader

SS-Oberführer Friedrich Panzinger

SS-Oberführer und Oberst der Polizei Dr Wilhelm Fuchs

Sonderkommando 1a: SS-Obersturmbannführer Dr Martin Sandberger followed by SS-Obersturmbannführer Bernhard Baatz.

Sonderkommando 1b: Erich Ehrlinger, Walter Hoffmann, Eduard Strauch, Erich Isselhorst.

Einsatzkommando 1a Martin Sandberger, Karl Tschierschky, Erich Isselhorst, Bernhard Baatz.

Einsatzkommando 1b: Hermann Hubig, Manfred Pechau.

Einsatzkommando 1c: Kurt Graaf.

Einsatzkommando 2: Rudolf Batz, Eduard Strauch, Rudolf Lange, Manfred Pechau, Reinhard Breder, Oswald Poche.

Einsatzkommando 3: Karl Jäger, Wilhelm Fuchs, Böhme.

Einsatzgruppe B

Attached to Army Group Centre.

Commanders: Arthur Nebe, Erich Naumann, Horst Bohme, Erich Ehrlinger, Heinrich Seetzen

Sonderkommando 7a

Operated: Vilna, Nevel, Vitebsk, Rzhev, Kalinin and Klintsy.

Commanders: Walter Blume, Eugen Steimle, Kurt Matschke, Albert Rapp, Helmut Looss, Gerhard Bast.

Sonderkommando 7b

Operated: Brest-Litovsk, Kobrin, Slonim, Baranovichi, Minst, Orsha, Briansk, Kursk and Orel.

Commanders: Günther Rausch, Adolf Ott, Josef Auinger, Karl-Georg Rabe.

Sonderkommando 7c

Operated: Moscow.

Commanders: Friedrich-Wilhelm Bock, Ernst Schmücker, Wilhelm Blühm, Hans Eckhardt.

Einsatzkommando 8

Operated: Volkovisk, Babruysk, Lahoysk, Mogilev and Minsk.

Commanders: Otto Bradfisch, Heinz Richter, Erich Isselhorst, Hans-Gerhard Schindhelm, Alfred Rendörffer.

Einsatzkommando 9

Operated: Vilna, Grodno, Lida, Bielsk-Podlaski, Nevel, Lepel, Surazh, Gzhatsk, Vitebsk, Smolensk and Varena.

Commanders: Alfred Filbert, Oswald Schafer, WilhelmWiebens, Friedrich Buchardt, Werner Kämpf.

Vorkommando Moskau

Operated: Moscow and Minsk area.

Commanders: Franz Six, Waldemar Klingelhofer, Erich Körting, Friedrich Buchardt, Friedrich-Wilhelm Bock.

Einzatzgruppe C

Attached to Army Group South.

Commanders: Otto Rasch, Max Thomas, Horst Bohme.

Einsatzkommando 4a

Operated: Lviv, Rovno, Lutsk, Pereyaslav, Ivankov, Radomyshl, Lubny, Jiev, Kursk and Kharkov.

Commanders: Paul Blobel, Erwin Weinmann, Eugen Steimle, Friedrich Schmidt, Theodor Christensen.

Einsatzkommando 4b

Operated: Lviv, Tranopol, Poltava, Sloviansk, Vinnytsia, Gorlovka, and Rostov.

Commanders: Gunther Herrmann, Fritz Braune, Walter Hänsch, August Meier, Friedrich Sühr, Waldemar Krause.

Einsatzkommando 5

Operated: Lviv, Brody, Dubno, Skvyra and Kiev.

Commanders: Erwin Schulz, August Meier.

Einsatzkommando 6

Operated: Lviv, Zolochiv, Zhytomyr, Proskurov, Vinnytsia, Kryvyi Rih, Stalino and Rostov.

Commanders: Erhard Kroger, Robert Möhr, Ernst Biberstein, Friedrich Sühr.

Einsatzgruppe D

Attached to the 11th Army.

Operated: northern Transylvania, Cernauti, Kishinev and Crimea area.

Commanders: Otto Ohlendorf, Walther Bierkamp.

Einsatzkommando 10a

Commanders: Heinrich Seetzen, Kurt Christmann.

Einsatzkommando 10b

Commanders: Alois Persterer, Eduard Jedamzik.

Einsatzkommando 11a

Commanders: Paul Zapp, Fritz Mauer, Gerhard Bast, Werner Hersmann.

Einsatzkommando 11b

Commanders: Hans Unglaube, Bruno Muller, Werner Braune, Paul Schultz.

Einsatzkommando 12

Commanders: Gustav Adolf Nosske, Erich Müller, Günther Herrmann.

Einsatzgruppe E

Operated: deployed in Croatia behind the 12th Army in the area of Vinkovci, Sarajevo, Banja, Luka, Knin and Zagreb.

Commanders: Ludwig Teichmann, Günther Herrmann, Wilhelm Fuchs.

Einsatzkommando 10b

Commanders: Joachim Deumling, Franz Sprinz.

Einsatzkommando 11a

Commanders: Rudolf Korndörfer, Anton Fest.

Einsatzkommando 15

Commander: Willi Wolter.

Einsatzkommando 16

Commanders: Johannes Thümmler, Joachim Freitag.

Einsatzkommando Agram

Commander: Rudolf Korndörfer.

Appendix 4

Number of people killed by the Einsatzgruppen

Figures from the Jäger and Stahlecker reports. People killed as of December 1942:

Einsatzgruppe A	363,337
Einsatzgruppe B	134,000
Einsatzgruppe C	118,341
Einsatzgruppe D	91,728
Higher SS, police leaders and staff	445,325

German Police Battalions and Regiments, 1939–44

The German police murdered over a million people in 1939–44. The following is only a selection of some the police battalions involved:

Police Battalion 1, Police Rifle Regiment 36
Formed 24 June 1943. Two battalions comprised of Ukrainian Schuma and personnel from Polish Regiment 8. Operations: Volozhin and Minsk.

Police Battalion 2
Formed Berlin 1 July 1942 from Polish Regiment 1. Operations: Reserve Polish Battalion 2 sent to Staraya Russa December 1941 to prevent a Red Army counter-offensive. Early 1942, south of Lake Ilmen, 3 April 1942 Dedovichi region to defend a railway line south from Leningrad toward Vitebsk. Eastern Poland April 1943, Holland July 1943.

Police Battalion 3
Formed Berlin July 1942 from Polish Regiment 1. Operations: Eastern Poland April 1943, Holland July 1943.

Police Battalion 6
Formed Berlin July 1942, part of Polish Regiment Nord. Became part of Polish Regiment 9. Destroyed 1944.

Police Battalion 9
Assigned to Einsatzgruppe D spring 1941, Einsatzgruppe 6, and Einsatzgruppe C in the Lemberg region

Police battalion 10
Operations: Eastern Poland April 1943, Holland July 1943.

Police Battalion 11
Formed Königsberg area July 1942 from Polish Regiment 2 Attached to Einsatzgruppe Slutsk in September 1941. Stationed in Kovno region from July 1941 and the 3rd Company guarded the Kovno ghetto. Operated alongside the 707 Security Division.

Police Battalion 12 F
Formed from parts of Polish Rifle Regiment in April 1943, three battalion-sized regiments. The 1st battalion was German, the other two comprised of Ukrainian

police units. Operations: 1st and 3rd Battalions operated in Pleshchenitsy near Borisov, 2nd Battalion saw action in Logoysk near Borisov. Disbanded summer 1944.

Police battalion 13

Formed in Konigsberg area July 1942 from Polish Regiment 2. Was attached to Einsatzgruppen in the Mlawa district in November 1942 Operations: Eastern Front winter 1943–44

Police Battalion 17

Formed from Polish Regiment 32 in April 1943. Reassigned as the I/Galizien Frewilligen Regiment 5

Police Battalion 20

Formed Police Rifle Regiment 33 in April 1943. The regiment's 1st and 2nd Battalions were Ukrainian Schuma.

Police Battalion 21

Formed Police Rifle Regiment 34 in April 1943. Operations: In 1943 and 1944 stationed in Bialystok. In 1943 used to crush the revolt in the Bialystok ghetto. In July 1944 it was sent to East Prussia. Later in 1944 sent to defend Warsaw. February–April 1945 became part of main defence in front of Berlin in Army Group Vistula.

Police Battalion 22

Battalion formed in Stettin area from Polish Regiment 2 in July 1942. Operations: Attached to the Einsatzgruppen for operations in Riga in late 1941; February 1943 Slutsk area.

Police battalion 23

Formed in Stettin area.

Police Battalion 24

Formed Police Rifle Regiment 35 in May 1943. Operations: Lodz in May 1943. Mid-summer sent to the Ukraine and saw action around Kiev area. At end of January 1944 was overrun by Soviet armour. February 1944, remnants moved to Dubno, but officially disbanded.

Police Battalion 32

Became part of Polish Regiment 21 July 1942, attached to Einsatzgruppen in Lvov September 1941. Operations: In July 1942 sent to Bruenn and then a year later to Moravia. In March 1944 the III/21 was sent to Hungary where in August it became the new Polish Regiment 1. The II/21 and III/21 saw defensive in action in Czechoslovakia in 1945.

Police Battalion 41

Raised in Leipzig, Dresden, Halle, Chemnitz. It formed Polish Regiment 22 July 1942. Operations: Eastern Front in White Russia, destroyed summer 1944. Disbanded December 1944 while defending Danzig.

Appendix 6

Executions carried out by Einsatzkommando 3
(from the Jäger report)

The following is a detailed report up to 1 December 1941 of Einsatzkommando 3 operations. It was part of Einsatzgruppe A.

The Commander of the security police
and the SD Einsatzkommando 3 Kauen [Kaunas],
1 December 1941

<u>Secret Reich Business!</u>
5 copies (4th copy)

Complete list of executions carried out in the EK 3 area up to 1 December 1941.

Security police duties in Lithuania taken over by Einsatzkommando 3 on 2 July 1941.

(The Wilna [Vilnius] area was taken over by EK 3 on 9 Aug. 1941, the Schaulen area on 2 Oct. 1941. Up until these dates EK 9 operated in Wilna and EK 2 in Schaulen.)

On my instructions and orders the following executions were conducted by Lithuanian partisans:

4.7.41	Kauen-Fort VII	416 Jews, 47 Jewesses	463
6.7.41	Kauen-Fort VII	Jews	2,514

Following the formation of a raiding squad under the command of SS-Obersturmführer Hamman and 8–10 reliable men from the Einsatzkommando, the following actions were conducted in cooperation with Lithuanian partisans:

7.7.41	Mariampole	Jews	32
8.7.41	Mariampole	14 Jews, 5 Comm. officials	19
8.7.41	Girkalinei	Comm. officials	6
9.7.41	Wendziogala	32 Jews, 2 Jewesses, 1 Lithuanian (f.), 2 Lithuanian Comm., 1 Russian Comm.	38
9.7.41	Kauen-Fort VII	21 Jews, 3 Jewesses	24
14.7.41	Mariampole	21 Jews, 1 Russ., 9 Lith. Comm.	31

Date	Place	Details	Count
17.7.41	Babtei	8 Comm. officials (incl. 6 Jews)	8
18.7.41	Mariampole	39 Jews, 14 Jewesses	53
19.7.41	Kauen-Fort VII	17 Jews, 2 Jewesses, 4 Lith. Comm., 2 Comm. Lithuanians (f.), 1 German Comm.	26
21.7.41	Panevezys	59 Jews, 11 Jewesses, 1 Lithuanian (f.), 1 Pole, 22 Lith. Comm., 9 Russ. Comm.	103
22.7.41	Panevezys	1 Jew	1
23.7.41	Kedainiai	83 Jews, 12 Jewesses, 14 Russ. Comm., 15 Lith. Comm., 1 Russ. O-Politruk	125
25.7.41	Mariampole	90 Jews, 13 Jewesses	103
28.7.41	Panevezys	234 Jews, 15 Jewesses, 19 Russ. Comm., 20 Lith. Comm.	288
29.7.41	Rasainiai	254 Jews, 3 Lith. Comm.	257
30.7.41	Agriogala	27 Jews, 11 Lith. Comm.	38
31.7.41	Utena	235 Jews, 16 Jewesses, 4 Lith. Comm., 1 robber/murderer	256
31.7.41	Wendziogala	13 Jews, 2 murderers	15
1.8.41	Ukmerge	254 Jews, 42 Jewesses, 1 Pol. Comm., 2 Lith. NKVD agents, 1 mayor of Jonava who gave order to set fire to Jonava	300
2.8.41	Kauen-Fort IV	170 Jews, 1 US Jewess, 33 Jewesses, 4 Lith. Comm.	209
4.8.41	Panevezys	362 Jews, 41 Jewesses, 5 Russ. Comm., 14 Lith. Comm.	422
5.8.41	Rasainiai	213 Jews, 66 Jewesses	279
7.8.41	Utena	483 Jews, 87 Jewesses, 1 Lithuanian (robber of corpses of German soldiers)	571
8.8.41	Ukmerge	620 Jews, 82 Jewesses	702
9.8.41	Kauen-Fort IV	484 Jews, 50 Jewesses	534
11.8.41	Panevezys	450 Jews, 48 Jewesses, 1 Lith. 1 Russ.	500
13.8.41	Alytus	617 Jews, 100 Jewesses, 1 criminal	719
14.8.41	Jonava	497 Jews, 55 Jewesses	552
15–16.8.41	Rokiskis	3,200 Jews, Jewesses, and J. Children, 5 Lith. Comm., 1 Pole, 1 partisan	3,207
9–16.8.41	Rasainiai	294 Jewesses, 4 Jewish children	298
27.6–14.8.41	Rokiskis	493 Jews, 432 Russians, 56 Lithuanians (all active communists)	981
18.8.41	Kauen-Fort IV	689 Jews, 402 Jewesses, 1 Pole (f.), 711 Jewish intellectuals from Ghetto in reprisal for sabotage action	1,812

19.8.41	Ukmerge	298 Jews, 255 Jewesses, 1 Politruk, 88 Jewish children, 1 Russ. Comm.	645
22.8.41	Dunanburg	3 Russ. Comm., 5 Latvian, incl. 1 murderer, 1 Russ. Guardsman, 3 Poles, 3 gypsies (m.), 1 gypsy (f.), 1 gypsy child, 1 Jew, 1 Jewess, 1 Armenian (m.), 2 Politruks (prison inspection in Dunanburg)	21
22.8.41	Aglona	Mentally sick: 269 men, 227 women, 48 children	544
23.8.41	Panevezys	1,312 Jews, 4,602 Jewesses, 1,609 Jewish children	7,523
18–22.8.41	Kreis Rasainiai	466 Jews, 440 Jewesses, 1,020 Jewish children	1,926
25.8.41	Obeliai	112 Jews, 627 Jewesses, 421 Jewish children	1,160
25–26.8.41	Seduva	230 Jews, 275 Jewesses, 159 Jewish children	664
26.8.41	Zarasai	767 Jews, 1,113 Jewesses, 1 Lith. Comm., 687 Jewish children, 1 Russ. Comm. (f.)	2,569
26.8.41	Kaisiadorys	All Jews, Jewesses, and Jewish children	1,911
27.8.41	Prienai	All Jews, Jewesses, and Jewish Children	1,078
27.8.41	Dagda and Kraslawa	212 Jews, 4 Russ. POWs	216
27.8.41	Joniskia	47 Jews, 165 Jewesses, 143 Jewish children	355
28.8.41	Pasvalys	402 Jews, 738 Jewesses, 209 Jewish children	1,349
28.8.41	Wilkia	76 Jews, 192 Jewesses, 134 Jewish children	402
28.8.41	Kedainiai	710 Jews, 767 Jewesses, 599 Jewish children	2,076
29.8.41	Rumsiskis and Ziezmariai	20 Jews, 567 Jewesses, 197 Jewish children	784
29.8.41	Utena and Moletai	582 Jews, 1,731 Jewesses, 1,469 Jewish children	3,782
13–31.8.41	Alytus and environs	233 Jews	233
1.9.41	Mariampole	1,763 Jews, 1,812 Jewesses, 1,404 Jewish children, 109 mentally sick, 1 German subject (f.), married to a Jew, 1 Russian (f.)	5,090
28.8–2.9.41	Darsuniskis	10 Jews, 69 Jewesses, 20 Jewish children	99
	Carliava	73 Jews, 113 Jewesses, 61 Jewish children	247
	Jonava	112 Jews, 1,200 Jewesses, 244 Jewish children	1,556
	Petrasiunai	30 Jews, 72 Jewesses, 23 Jewish children	125
	Jesuas	26 Jews, 72 Jewesses, 46 Jewish children	144
	Agriogala	207 Jews, 260 Jewesses, 195 Jewish children	662
	Jasvainai	86 Jews, 110 Jewesses, 86 Jewish children	282
	Babtei	20 Jews, 41 Jewesses, 22 Jewish children	83
	Wendziogala	42 Jews, 113 Jewesses, 97 Jewish children	252
	Krakes	448 Jews, 476 Jewesses, 97 Jewish children	1,125

4.9.41	Pravenischkis	247 Jews, 6 Jewesses	253
	Cekiske	22 Jews, 64 Jewesses, 60 Jewish children	146
	Seredsius	6 Jews, 61 Jewesses, 126 Jewish children	193
	Velinona	2 Jews, 71 Jewesses, 86 Jewish children	159
	Zapiskis	47 Jews, 118 Jewesses, 13 Jewish children	178
5.9.41	Ukmerge	1,123 Jews, 1,849 Jewesses, 1,737 Jewish children	4,709
25.8–6.9.41	Mopping up in:		
	Rasainiai	16 Jews, 412 Jewesses, 415 Jewish children all	843
	Georgenburg	Jews, all Jewesses, all Jewish children	412
9.9.41	Alytus	287 Jews, 640 Jewesses, 352 Jewish children	1,279
9.9.41	Butrimonys	67 Jews, 370 Jewesses, 303 Jewish children	740
10.9.41	Merkine	223 Jews, 640 Jewesses, 276 Jewish children	854
10.9.41	Varena	541 Jews, 141 Jewesses, 149 Jewish children	831
11.9.41	Leipalingis	60 Jews, 70 Jewesses, 25 Jewish children	155
11.9.41	Seirijai	229 Jews, 384 Jewesses, 340 Jewish children	953
12.9.41	Simnas	68 Jews, 197 Jewesses, 149 Jewish children	414
11–12.9.41	Uzusalis	Reprisal against inhabitants who fed Russ. partisans; some in possession of weapons	43
26.9.41	Kauen-F.IV	412 Jews, 615 Jewesses, 581 Jewish children (sick and suspected epidemic cases)	1,608
2.10.41	Zagare	633 Jews, 1,107 Jewesses, 496 Jewish children (as these Jews were being led away a mutiny rose, which was however immediately put down; 150 Jews were shot immediately; 7 partisans wounded)	2,236
4.10.41	Kauen-F.IX	315 Jews, 712 Jewesses, 818 Jewish children (reprisal: German police officer shot in ghetto)	1,845
29.10.41	Kauen-F.IX	2,007 Jews, 2,920 Jewesses, 4,273 Jewish children (mopping up ghetto of superfluous Jews)	9,200
3.11.41	Lazdijai	485 Jews, 511 Jewesses, 539 Jewish children	1,535
15.11.41	Wilkowiski	36 Jews, 48 Jewesses, 31 Jewish children	115
25.11.41	Kauen-F.IX	1,159 Jews, 1,600 Jewesses, 175 Jewish children (resettlers from Berlin, Munich, Frankfurt am main)	2,934
29.11.41	Kauen-F.IX	693 Jews, 1,155 Jewesses, 152 Jewish children (resettlers from from Vienna and Breslau)	2,000
29.11.41	Kauen-F.IX	17 Jews, 1 Jewess, for contravention of ghetto law, 1 Reichs German who converted to the Jewish faith and attended rabbinical school, then 15 terrorists from the Kalinin group	34

EK 3 detachment in Dunanburg in the period
13.7–21.8.41:   9,012 Jews, Jewesses and Jewish children,   9,585
                                 573 active Comm.

EK 3 detachment in Wilna:
12.8–1.9.41   City of Wilna   425 Jews, 19 Jewesses, 8 Comm. (m.),   461
                                 9 Comm. (f.)
2.9.41   City of Wilna   864 Jews, 2,019 Jewesses, 817 Jewish children   3,700
                                 (sonderaktion: German soldiers shot at by Jews)
12.9.41   City of Wilna   993 Jews, 1,670 Jewesses, 771 Jewish children   3,334
17.9.41   City of Wilna   337 Jews, 687 Jewesses, 247 Jewish children and 1,271
                                 4 Lith. Comm.
20.9.41   Nemencing   128 Jews, 176 Jewesses, 99 Jewish children   403
22.9.41   Novo-Wilejka   468 Jews, 495 Jewesses, 196 Jewish children   1,159
24.9.41   Riess   512 Jews, 744 Jewesses, 511 Jewish children   1,767
25.9.41   Jahiunai   215 Jews, 229 Jewesses, 131 Jewish children   575
27.9.41   Eysisky   989 Jews, 1,636 Jewesses, 821 Jewish children   3,446
30.9.41   Trakai   366 Jews, 483 Jewesses, 597 Jewish children   1,446
4.10.41   City of Wilna   432 Jews, 1,115 Jewesses, 436 Jewish children   1,983
6.10.41   Semiliski   213 Jews, 359 Jewesses, 390 Jewish children   962
9.10.41   Svenciany   1,169 Jews, 1,840 Jewesses, 717 Jewish children 3,726
16.10.41   City of Wilna   382 Jews, 507 Jewesses, 257 Jewish children   1,146
21.10.41   City of Wilna   718 Jews, 1,063 Jewesses, 586 Jewish children   2,367
25.10.41   City of Wilna   1,776 Jewesses, 812 Jewish children   2,578
27.10.41   City of Wilna   946 Jews, 184 Jewesses, 73 Jewish children   1,203
30.10.41   City of Wilna   382 Jews, 789 Jewesses, 362 Jewish children   1,553
6.11.41   City of Wilna   340 Jews, 749 Jewesses, 252 Jewish children   1,341
19.11.41   City of Wilna   76 Jews, 77 Jewesses, 18 Jewish children   171
19.11.41   City of Wilna   6 POWs, 8 Poles   14
20.11.41   City of Wilna   3 POWs   3
25.11.41   City of Wilna   9 Jews, 46 Jewcsses, 8 Jewish children, 1 Pole for 64
                                 possession of arms and other military equipment

EK 3 detachment in Minsk from
28.9–17.10.41   Pleschnitza,   620 Jews, 1,285 Jewesses, 1,126 Jewish children 3,050
                 Bischolin,   and 19 Comm.
                 Scak, Bober,
                 Uzda

                                                                               133,346
Prior to EK 3 taking over security police duties, Jews liquidated by pogroms and   4,000
executions (including partisans)

                                                                    Total   137,346

Notes

Notes

Notes